the night
i dropped shakespeare
on the cat

john olson

The Night I Dropped Shakespeare on the Cat

© 2006 John Olson

ISBN 0-9770723-3-9

Cover design and illustrations by Derek White.

Title page, contents, and title fonts by Eduardo Recife.

Grateful thanks go out to the following publications in which some of these pieces first appeared: *The Absinthe Literary Review, Bewildering Stories, Bird Dog, Call, Cranky, First Intensity, Knock, New American Writing, The Raven Chronicles, Sentence: A Journal of Prose Poetics, Sleepingfish, Talisman, Traverse, Unarmed,* and *Wandering Hermit*.

Published by Calamari Press, New York, NY

www.calamaripress.com

contents

4

For Roberta, and our cat Toby, whose purring
soliloquies tender the weight of Shakespeare

Delinquent Circuitry

A volt is having a since to glint. Nimble to town. Summer soon ceiling. A bee beside the knife. Catalogue of auburn. Wood as a word as a smudge as a snap as a seismic creamery. A blister, or bluster. A bag of nails jaw full of vowels jar full of babble. An equation which causes damask by adherence and hull. An idea broiled in thought. A scab articulate as property. Real estate is ravenous with borders. An escalator among the fiddlers encouraging ascendancy to an alphabet made of weight and fur and electrically charged particles. Each sound is packed in straw. Endocrine money. Experience irritated into silver. Extremities of meaning rattled in rhinoceros ink. Ambergris consonants. Occurrences of unbridled world excited by tin. A sun of crazily wiggling fingers rising out of a rule of thumb. Smile you're on candid bareback. Godiva with a hammer. If I had a hammer a hammer and a nail I would build an epiglottis for swallows. A hive of irregularities. And a poem of ocher and jute. Judicious evaporation. Baubles of flash and cowlick. A democracy imposed on living cells of impolitic smirk Reno in February a mist of sweeping ambiguity coddled in tumultuous cognition a raw career of cactus and dimes soaked in conviction a black chair a contusion winking with ore a feeling for rust the nectar of scientific data upsetting a capital. Do you seek meaning and wisdom in a poem? I seek the occurrence of sound in protein. In propulsion. In bas-relief. The real estate of pleasure which is a perfectly red abstraction accelerating green again and again on a brawl of bronze.

Tools

When I think of tools I think of tools and thinking becomes a tool. This proves that insects are Gothic. If we need a stage on which to enact life, the citrus of the sitar makes clothes appear to be 50 degrees Fahrenheit. Some bodies look natural in space and others are nude and unobtainable. The nipple serves as an apparatus for precipitating rubber. The process is episcopal and matt.

We send messages to one another via barrels full of glue. Each soldier carries a blanket and a lily.

We establish an intricate polyphonic structure by focusing on a screw and inserting the screw in the proper hole and hoping it stays there long enough to get the tip of the screwdriver blade into the slot on the head of the screw before it falls out. Later, when the counterpoint unfolds, an allegro in E-flat jerks us forward like kleptomaniacs at a hardware store, purging our darker impulses with simple nurturing confrontations, such as maligning a checker for keeping us waiting in line too long.

Cryogenic sedans patrol the back roads looking for Scandinavia. Hunger, poverty, and illness are there to help us to understand linoleum.

How supple is the human tongue when it is driven on two wheels!

Materialism matters to metal. Potassium compensates for ballet. If we are unhappy with a daydream, we turn it into a ceremony. The internal circuitry of the table saw makes Christmas jell in our arms like a neck turning infrared. As a life travels through various bedrooms, it spirals around a central idea called buckles.

Women undress in small rooms above the saloon.

Whatever happened to the nickelodeon?

A sentence is generated when it gets around to growing into aspen. If postulated as a principle of universal grammar, it can explain why the forsythia is subject to changing moods, and oak is thick and idealism is thicker, concealing and revealing the body with weightlessness and pie.

Meaning is a tool for the preternaturally fat. For one thing, it is young and pretty and hard to come by. The meaning of this is that a sentence is an igloo floating through a fairground stuffed with magnetos and maps. Hedda Gabler, dressed to receive callers, is alone in the room. A propeller is spinning like a rotisserie chicken, and garlic and touch propose many different ways to express liquid. It is therefore an error to consider the igloo a strictly temporal concern, but a mode of thought contrasting areas of light and shade with the final pronouncement of the subject by the trumpet, a cantata dreaming of itself as water.

Consonants Cracked in Allegory

There is a stick among the bricks that rotates in such a way as to invite insects to battle anonymity. Nickel such words as they undulate in meaning. The deep lamp of urbanity will thrust its light on the hand's blister, making it sugary and transparent. Horrified, kind, and flavor hard. A raw naked hole of sudden canary. There is a scab on the macaroni that ad-libs fervor with its phantom stamina. The thong of the thought is a cormorant I'm nuts about. I would nod to the day as it rose in the east in its binocular smelt. A chutney library badgering change with its windows and fog sobs and bumps against the false appearances of theatre in a dollar bill, resulting in winter. A bagpipe however alpaca should never be carried to the carnival. Glance at the brown and smash that anthem to consonants of California sunlight. An underwater eyeball rattling with suntans. One day we will construct an ode out of new participles, most of them mirrors, a few of them blade-like correlatives sharp as a hawk on an oasis drum. It is so all estuaries are iron that a language means its antiques to reside in metal tongues. By elastic they mean the night might quake or break apart on an orchid. It is necessary to solve the rattlesnake by Wednesday. Live up to the fact of courage as if everyone's face were a bell sounding evaporation on a raft. Essence means micas are living and all the reindeer on television will batter themselves against the screen causing rainbows of experience to reverberate on the ceilings and fables. There are affections in the abacus no one has yet considered to verify. The octave is an ornament of sound but a moccasin is sweet to the skin. Each character has a glaze, a sweetly curving leg that moves with the abandon of fire. A Peru ravenous in its daily flap.

A Bee is a Predicate with Wings

Everything we see in this world we see in sequence. Sequins. A chain of events. A necklace of noise. Succession. Series. Strings and upshots. Cause and effect. Spanish motorcyclists tumbling through the air.

Venus passing before the sun.

Red velour Christmas bow tied to a black wrought iron step rail.

Christ bearing the cross.

Two men hoisting a mattress up a flight of steps.

A ring of neon tubes lighting up white and brilliant in systematic, mesmerizing waves around and around the circle.

Women's nylons both revealing and concealing the flesh and tone and shape of a leg.

Gravestones capped in snow.

A man in a gray jacket balancing rocks on a Puget Sound breaker while an Elliott Bay gull looks on from an adjacent rock.

Pops wheezes coughs hiccups. Muscle and skin leaving footprints on a beach.

There is reality in shape, shape in reality. Fables, blisters, flint. Meat and coincidence.

A word is nothing without contingency. Hawk on a nickelodeon.

Some things bend. Some things bead. If you watch a living amoeba under a microscope you will see squiggles. Division. Reproduction. Contingency.

Events sequenced in time hold the air in place. Lumber and nail eventually become a barn. A stable. A momentary space. The heady odor of hay and manure. The dazzle of beams. The harnessing of time.

When something moves we call it a narration. A story.

Light through a lens, images on a screen.

An eyeball is a globe of water. It exemplifies jam. Something inside that little speck of jelly thinks circumference is appealing. And thereby hangs a volume.

Narration mutilates space. Creatures called words develop eyes and articulations to give meaning to the invisible world. Thought, design, ligament.

There is sometimes a moment so great and heady it seems everything is on the verge of bursting. And then it does. It bursts. Remnants of luminous color come dropping down in slow biography. And there you are face to face with the great mystery. Everything falls into place and a door opens. A door to what? A farm in the 1500s. An autumn in nineteenth century France. Ecuador crinkled and imposing on a Spanish map.

It is the characteristic of an eye to validate the visible and see who or what has been in the room. Each room is a story. We live inside ourselves. We live inside our narratives with furniture and people and paintings. Thought is the furniture of the mind and philosophy is the facing surface of our camera obscura. Everything ham and hammered and holy and happening is outside in the visible world. It becomes allegory in the invisible world. It becomes ogres and jungles and phantoms and amulets. It becomes December. It becomes taxis and thermostats. Thesis and sunspots. This is how the invisible is made visible. An aperture in the mind dilates into orchards and monkeyshines. Resolute buccaneers. Rope and canvas. Mermaids. Fiddles. Verbs.

We see through a seeing. We see through a seeing into a seeming sea of storms and asterisks. And as imagination bodies forth the forms of things unknown, the poet's pen turns them to shapes, and gives to airy nothing a local habitation and a name.

One must start with luggage, symbols varnished with the lacquer of thought.

It is very hard to hold a marble udder on a granite cow. But you can milk it once you become familiar with the beauty of extravagance. A story is, after all, a hunt. A pursuit. Twilight beaten into tinfoil. A face reflected in a lake.

Pollen. Pewter. Breakfast at Tiffany's.

Each sentence is an intrigue, an alias, a din. Can you hear that?

A bee is a predicate with wings.

Each noun shakes loose a host of possibility. A Kansas marshal in baggy clothes. Pistons of rain moving a tangle of words into motion and shape.

Jacks are the tangible evidences of life. Who at one time or another has not pulled a jack from a trunk and wondered how it works. Wondered if it is even the right jack. And pulled the implement all dusty and puzzling out of the trunk and set it down on the road and pondered it and tried to figure its narrative out in the mind before getting one's fingers and thumb pinched in getting the thing set up under the car.

No narrative can work without a spare tire, a feeling for wheels and formulation. A reverence for engines, bright silver sheen of the street when the December sun pops out. An elephant in the rearview mirror.

If you want to build a mask of damask you must do so brick by brick. This is what we do in fiction. We signify caulk with a caulking gun and wipe away the excess with a moist T-shirt.

A story begins with a heading. It is mappable by apple and glaze. It is already in our scheme of things quivering like a flame in our personal conception of eternity.

Feeling tired? Low self-esteem? Light a candle. Take a bath in rose petals.

Imagine Idaho. The rapids are sizzling with suspense. The water crawls or bounces over the rocks in a cantata of liquid rhetoric because it is the way our minds foam out of our heads. We go inward for scenes of our inner life as if the mind were a theatre. We watch the curtain rise on a jeep. A colossal eyeball floats overhead. We search for coordinates and find meaning in barrels of peanuts and creaking floors. When we open our eyes we find that the rapids are still there, but appear different, more copulative and silver in flashes of fractious splendor.

We know what it is to row and row and make a narration of rowing, a tale of endocrine and flags where viewpoint is the seed of plot and the water beneath us causes our convictions to float, unanimous in movement. Believe me this is so. Think of resolution as a form of ambergris, a residue left by vagaries of implication and gray.

The wisdom of feelings drive the narration through fragments of hindsight and recall, Ray Charles and Clint Eastwood sharing a piano bench talking about the blues. October broken into bits of hue, pancakes heaped on a plate in Topeka.

What happened that day with the spoon? Why was there so much pressure to order? Why was the menu so large and cold to the touch?

The waitress was friendly and thin and appeared to be in her early forties. She was energetic and friendly. And yet there was a hint of melancholy in her carriage, a soupçon of thirst only time could quench. But whose story was that, hers, or our own? Were we reading too much into her facial expressions, her manner of walking, her general demeanor? Were we projecting our own personal narrative onto someone else? Was the pork chop cooked enough? The mashed potatoes mashed enough? Why did the sugar come in packets when the salt was allowed its own bottle at the table?

The first tales were told by tinkling sunlight in the left knee while juggling bits of air called words. Rhinoceroses, bears, deer, bison, wild horses, oxen, boars. Necks, locks, water skis, needles, periscopes, resurrections, sarongs.

I have never had a gun aimed at me. This, somehow, seems essential to a full existence, to have one's life held in balance like that, by a stranger, by someone who could care less about you, all they want is your money, what a terrific attitude would emerge from such an experience, and yet, in the very process of writing about it, am I in some way bringing it on? Do words cause things to happen?

The story is a balance between caissons and caviar. Thoughts and ideas flushed from the skull engraved with the fauna of a vanished world.

People live in two worlds, a nebulous brochure of postponed aspirations and a narcotic flexibility. Inner world visions are more vivid than real life. They pulse with harmonicas and boulevards. Snow in the streets turning to slush. Bright chartreuse moss splotched on a concrete retaining wall. A cage for savage emotions. Tambourines. Feathers for strange rituals.

Devotion is an animal. It is the reason for nudes. We are but the servants of a world we cannot see, a world of light and joy, Beale Street in 1953.

A pair of old jeans tossed and crumpled on a lamentable couch.

Duck decoys circling a birdbath. Axioms and dots. Sand as far as the eye can see.

There is no complete reality without hearing it, tasting it, feeling it, weighing it, sewing it together with words and intuitions, circuitry and levers.

Pearls on a horse. Candy on a radio.

It is vital to have something our senses can grasp and suck into our being, a lamp or a color, a ramification tasting of cod. The intangible pattern of reality adheres to our alphabet like twilight, thought inflated with noble gases.

Everything is a frontier. I say everything is a frontier. The most familiar thing in the world is a frontier. If it is not a frontier you have not looked at it properly. What is the most familiar thing to you? Your hand? Your arm? Your embroidery? Is it the way water evaporates? Is it a field where something or someone is buried?

The American frontier makes better sense on the other side of a patent misunderstanding. Imagine a town of phantoms, a village dripping with violins. Iodine and pulleys. The smell of a garage. The bright succulence of words. Patina, animus, stain. A sentence rough and frayed and hung obliquely on a towel rack.

An afghan, a watermark, an alcove.

New Year's confetti on the sidewalk. Cord winding down from an electric drill. Black Diamond. Rut in a muddy street. A bronze crucifixion by Bernini.

Jewelry in a cedar bureau. Fine sand fanned out at the bottom of the sidewalk.

Water beaded on the window of a Shanghai train. A man punching paint into a canvas. Orchid trembling slightly as someone rushes by. Research. Butter. Mastic.

That's it. That's what a story does. It fabricates an atmosphere then opens it with rain.

Universe of Words

Lets dinghy the words to grapple them readily. For instance, listen and glisten. Fleet, feet, and salamander. That color tinges the dragon with so much caffeine it crackles. It flies up to the cage to knit a tattoo. As a flap of rawhide distinguishes the west, a flash of dragon distinguishes mood. The mood of havoc. The mood of scale. A lambent mood of harmony infects the eccentricity of crows. Even the human face will sometimes crash through a crust of hydrogen emitting proverbs and saws. Space itself is pitched into the salad of night while lines of poetry bubble with diphthongs. It takes a genuine helium to yeast along the edge of Thursday. Calling itself a form of slowness, a jar of mayonnaise languishes in a Japanese cellar. It was once a bikini that celebrated lassitude, but since the advent of a divine éclair it is a mound of sage in a spoon that conjures so much understanding of daydreams and bandstands. Until the architecture of winter caused the pleasure of borscht to expand into language we had no way to effectively measure the rhetoric of being. Being is an effluent that's ravenous to intone. We know that much. We also know that discovery is entrenched in width until such time that schools begin to open in autumn and orchestras resume their seats near the front of the stage. A reddish-brown membrane yells pink at a buxom woman stretching into her sweat. This reminds us of snowshoes and sushi. A mow that whittles the pumpkin is mow mow than a muu-muu on a Mau-Mau, or an apple in a box of apricots. Move your body near the crocodile to search the electricity of counsel. Geometry houses squirrels. Most of our rangers are able to see them turn exponential near the arcade. Our universe is made of bullets and tubas. How it is nailed to the backbone of an alphabet I cannot say.

The germination of such poetry will take a while. Lagniappe is definitely bold as the machinery stands still. Even those imponderable cobblestones of corduroy inflate with cognition when alliteration is added to the crosswalk. You might call this a universe of words, a sun's death doing its origins again as an irritant, or herring. The noise of this is a scratched engine, a personal stem of bombast dwelling forever in identity. Tendencies to create a personality out of buttons and gears shimmies toward a whole bell of teakettle facts, a cauldron of knobs and leaves we call Halloween. Abstraction is our main pursuit this time of year, our best means of securing goldenrod in beauty. That's why so much effort is made to permeate the air with words. If all the lemonade is alchemically whole, why not add the precision of a bean?

Unconscious

One must not forget the unconscious. The unconscious is full of delectable monstrosities. Odysseys and octopus and the fat dangling udders of soluble fish. It is a massa confusa. It is a fat pink bailiff on a catwalk. It is a director's cut. It is a demonstrable aching desire.

The unconscious is an escalator on the inner thigh of a fourteen year-old girl.

Going up and down and up and down and up and down.

You get the picture.

Such is the nature of the unconscious. Bring a flashlight if you go there. Bring a flashlight and a map and a bag of potato chips. Because friend, we are entering the realm of the imagination, the dark cavernous region where the imagination begins, down there, down there at the base of your brain, there in the limbic region, there in the limbo region, the place of shadows, the place of big wet slimy things, the place of vengeance and the place of rage, the place of tenderness and the place of sighs, the hall of ringing fury, the hall of Vulcan, the hall of the Lizard King.

Ride the snake. Ride the snake to the lake. The ancient lake. The snake is long, seven miles. Ride the snake. He's old, and his skin is cold.

Two giant salamanders guard the door to the Hall of Sunsets. There in the Hall of Sunsets you will find laudanum and orange and tinctures of death. Sweet death, sweet oblivion.

One word and all comes back to life again.

One word and all rises into being like blood in the neck.

Rises from the unconscious. Which is a place in the brain. Which is a warm place. A warm place full of blood. And convolution. And imaginary realms like the unconscious. Which is a word. Which is a viscous wedge of biology. Attached to a sentence. Which it needs for sustenance, and life. And chewing.

Chewing and chewing and chewing. A life of chewing. And death and decay and fetid swamps. That, too, is part of the unconscious. That region in the brain. That region that Freud and Jung gave a name. And so there it is: the pretty arch of a woman's foot dangling in front of a coffeehouse.

The drug of writing gives birth to things other than children.

Think of phantoms.

Think of a girl with long black hair and red pants sitting on a rock. Leaves trembling, a shadow moving back and forth on a picnic table.

It is a curious thing.

Soft Pedaling a Thesis of Scabs

Coating the fable of clocks has been a gentle geography I can pedal around the house brandishing sentiments of catastrophic brocade. Writing it makes it thicken. Thought juggles moons. An immersion in nickelodeons. Jade and character shape the understanding of fish as one by one a balloon drifts by dragging examples of string. It is near my knot to abrade a Wednesday for tolerating banks. That's not the right place to put your money. The right place to put your money is in a mechanical sonnet made of onyx and reverie. The contortion of syntax is natural to a sonnet where thought occurs as a species of evergreen, a shrub whose foliage smells of arousal and art. Equations of lust engraved in gut. It is mere folderol to say the guitar gives sound a feeling of night. How ideal to wade through brass singing of silver. Writing is silver when it stops at nothing but adhesion. It is in the spirit of adhesion to stick to something. And so uniforms offend the amenity of black. Noon pencils itself into the research of trout. Trout are the ambassadors of noon. Sable is the ambassador of night. The machinery of representation pulls bathtubs out of hats and artificial intelligence out of cellos. Sequins carillons and paste. Sunlight barracuda and taste. The rainbow is a form of baroque secretion shreds of air sewn into bands of color with a pot of gold at each end struggling to achieve some modicum of viability within a context of miscreant declension. An arch of words crashing down on the hills. Words riveted to paper. Words sprinkled on paper. A treatise of mood treated to resin, jasmine, and plaid.

Maps

It is easy to find twenty maps and go there. A map of Berlin a map of China a map of California a map of yawning a map of requisitions. A map of pallets a map of palettes a map of palates a map of pellets a map of palominos. A map of overflowing personalities. A map of carpentry a map of choruses singing a song about faucets. A map of faucets in a faucet factory. A map of autumn. A map of winter. A map of summer effervescing hills. A map of spring redeeming gypsum. A map of rawhide a map of junctions a map of prepositions palpable as lipstick. A map of understanding obtruding handstands. A map of rock 'n roll black with scales. A map of eyebrows rendered in feathers. A map of clouds trapped in rhubarb. A map of thought loosened in tights. A map of breezes saturated with abstraction. A map of absorption absorbed in absence. A map of belief anchored in speculation. A map of unattachment attached to Atchison. A map of Düsseldorf soaked in cologne. A map of language assaulted by ink. A map of fever faced with moonlight. A map of moonlight imprinted in leather. A map of emotion trimmed with weather. If all the maps of everything mapped were rolled into orchids I would know where to go to find rapids. Hammers and snakes and South America. A map of entrances a map of exits. The map of exits is left on a streetcar. A map of smoke is found in a fire. A choice of maps is an indication of glass. Glass and spectral arias. An aria is an area of song and is mapped in muscle, resonance, and wire. A map of mops is made of strands. A map of time is made of hands. A map of limbo lingers in incubation. A map of warmth is crimson and bright. If you need a map of Isaac Newton or Eugene O'Neill the best place to look is in gravity, reaction, or journey long into the night.

City of Water

I live in a city of water. Water in all its forms. Vapor, clouds, drizzle. Fountains, rivers, lakes. Inlets, ports, sounds. There is water everywhere. Water has shaped and bathed and baffled the city. There is water to drink and water to boil. Water glittering and deep. Water glittering and wide. Water quivering and radiant and sympathetic to the philosophy of immersion. Water turquoise and green. Water with the complexion of smoldering topaz. Water to break water to wash water to enact in Elizabethan costume. Water to map water to absorb water to arrange with tubs and names. Duwamish. Shilshole. Sammamish. Water permeable as Beethoven and convincing as mud. Wherever you go in the city you cannot escape it. You can only surrender to the fact of it. The ubiquity of it. Its omnipresence and moss. Water parceled in berries. Water full of nuance and mallards and waves. Water in bogs. Water in bags. Water in guns. Water squirted into the face. Water under pressure water circulating a labyrinth of pipes. Water filtered through faucets water adjusted in nozzles. Water tumbled in the mind in images of rock and convulsion. Water in my body. Water around my body. Water in spit water in thumbs and eyeballs. Water punctuating the earth with commas. Puddles promiscuous as nickels. Puddles impertinent as pickles. Water streaked with whorls of delinquent oil. Everywhere the sheen and luster of water. Rivers in reveries of water. Water pushed to extremes. Water falling from cliffs. Water sprayed over melons. Water in beads on the blade of a fern. Water in rivulets on a window. Water impelling a current water moving in a kind of languor water moving reflectively from rock to rock. Word to word. Petal to petal. Collecting in pools. In limpidity. Water wiggled under a Buddha in jade.

The Fabric of Fabrication

If I say snail what do you see? Do you see a small mollusk with a spiral shell as the dictionary describes? Do you see a trail of slime? Moss? Lichen? The contingent debris of a summer morning? How is this possible?

And if I say the snail is made of glass and powered by a small machine of bearings and chains what do you see? Is the snail palpable to you? Is it clear? Is it ambiguous? Does it make a sound? Refute the empire of the real with an illusion of mechanical life?

How glib and easy it is to go from image to image leaving a trail of glistening significance. But whose significance? Mine, or yours?

All meaning balances on an image. A horizon, a signal, a bruise. The image, any image, compels apprehension of something larger than a sock, or complexion. Reflection on the image immediately poses the question from what is the image made? What does it represent? What is there to indicate the image is in rapport with something tangible, something actual, with whatever it is to which it refers, of which it is the supposed sign or symbol, its specular double?

The mind is a camera obscura, a chamber into which light passes, casting an image of luminous opulence on our personal screen. The image refers, we believe, to a primary reality. It is taken for granted. But therein lies the problem. Because the reality the image is presumed to reveal or unveil is obscured by that selfsame image. It would require the grandeur of delirium to break it apart. Because the image veils, in some sense, what it reveals. It is a multiplication of the object, a primary doubling, that allows something to be figured, to be abstracted into pearls of cognitive luster.

Society's arrogant certainties infect us, distort our perception. The paramount task of the artist is to rip these assumptions apart so that reality may be more immediately grasped. So that we see what is truly out there. An orchid in the Congo, bottles of balm loaded on a pallet in Guam, chunks of shark meat tossed on a scale in Madagascar. The Ambassador Of Butterflies leaving his hotel with a swarm of monarchs and a purple umbrella. Mozart with a quill in his hand. A black lamp dropping its light on the surface of a mahogany desk.

A mirror is never entirely innocent of reality. But sometimes the face it reflects belongs to a stranger. A face we continue to shave, or daub with makeup, even though it is the face of someone we are not quite sure of, someone we have known since birth but whose feelings and perceptions are sometimes so odd and unexpected that it cannot belong to us. We cannot account for the expression, the look, the beard, the mustache, the mascara, that apparatus of muscle and hair called a face. Is that face my face? How did it come to look so old? It does not match the image in my mind.

Art is the hacksaw by which we work at removing our bars. The prison of our assumptions.

There is the special appeal, the special smell and feel of rope, that can offer a figure, a truth of sorts, or absorption. Perceptions tend to wallow in promiscuity. They will seize anything out of which to construct some rigging, hoist some sail into the air. A statement to sail us into someone's affections. Or tack contrary to an opinion and fire a cannon into a penumbra of hostile supposition. Bluster, insolence, pomposity.

What we can say of the world is this: it is big and round and full of detail. When one sense mingles with another sense we lose sense of one world and gain sense of another world. A world where colors smell of music and music flashes carmine and gold. An expanse of sleeping water awakens into ripples of emerald. Sometimes reality will seep through an image and cause it to sprawl into Shakespeare like a forest or fable. Toe, rhythm, hand. Rust, tactic, tang.

An image is a constructed signification, trout leaping from a symbolist poem, rainbow dripping words. We can change our politics but we cannot change jade into anchovies or anchovies into jade. When we construct a sentence a chain of events is put into motion, each word treated like a jujube, a chewable sweetness, a green and propulsive goo leading to an ideology, notions of meaning, ideas of creation, equations written on a blackboard.

A hand is of particular interest. It has fingers, an opposable thumb, lines on the palm. A legible map for the fortune teller, a bundle of muscle for the tennis player. One believes only what one sees. But put an object in the hand and a sense of miracle baffles the skin. The squirm of a toad. The smooth sleep of a piece of paper.

A man cannot run down a runway without causing a little chaos. Who is this guy? Is it you? Is it me? Minutes later we find ourselves back at the airport pondering the sparkles on a bottle of mineral water. No image is an isolated event but a jukebox full of songs from the 60s. Paint It Black. Eleanor Rigby. House of the Rising Sun.

There is a country of the mind where reflection is a pure and tranquil thing, a pump on the Dakota prairie, a bronze sun on a silver background. Images don't enter the mind without some mediating agency. Jet engines fired up as the wing flaps are tested, the sun just beginning to pierce a layer of overcast, light diffused through a spread of gray. The sky compels us to look upwards and persuade us there is another much higher world. It is, therefore, an image of solace, though its reality might be something altogether different. At 30,000 feet, the world below is a sonnet. A realm of couplets and groves. Aphoristic hedges and clever streets. Religious feelings grow into parables. And then the plane lands, and we discover the world is terminally chromatic, a place of intervals and modes, feelings of vagueness given mathematical energy, the Rose Festival queens with their honorary titles leading to exponential loquacity, the 17th century Dutch painters assuming an importance they did not have before, we were so captivated by Roman shields, a queer silence jingled by a telephone.

I once played wide receiver for the Minnesota Vikings. Plays were represented as shotguns and wishbones, formations and red zones. This was our reality. But the reality of this reality was biology: bone impacting bone. Muscle opposing muscle. Reality, being too thorny for my great personality, I sought refuge in the compelling world of cartoons. Here, we take it on faith that what is there is there, that there is a reality to Superman's cape, that the world perceived through our five senses is fragmented and incomplete and made whole again in the comic. Our perception of the world is an act of faith based on fragments, images carved out of the air by poets, reckless assaults on reality sustained in the imagination by the mesmerizing swagger of rock stars.

Every time we see a photograph reproduced in a newspaper or magazine, our eyes take in the fragmented, black-and-white image of the half-tone patterns and our minds translate it into reality.

The image is assumed to be synonymous with reality. Snags and shoals in the Mississippi river, coconuts in an allegory painted by Paul Gauguin, the skeleton of a whale found washed ashore in Long Beach, Washington are all curiously completed in our mind as a landscape or nebular world, that personal wallpaper we call a gestalt. A tract of ground surrounding our head with celery. Celerity. A story expressing hardship. Ribbons. Begonias. The smell of money.

What images arise in the word 'January'?

A mood embodied in wood. Darkness smashed into light.

It is in the nature of perception to reach for an object and call it an absorption, an abstraction dressed in asterisks. A garden hose sprawled out on a parking lot, a pelican perched on a rock. A river passing over a vagary of pebbles, a bottle of iodine in a medicine cabinet. An island on the far horizon. A badge pinned to a marshal's vest.

I forget what fog means. Did fog mean something?

Mirrors upon mirrors, distortions in a funhouse. The world is never completely available, but there are multiple ways of looking at things. Feelings are large because they swell into algebra, funny equations, parallels, analogies, new enactments, as if the poem were a cockpit, a pamphlet of plums in a laboratory of words.

We make judgments based on nothing but thoughts, and what are they? Mountains and cockatoos. The furniture of the mind where reality is put into play between shadows and light. Gravity hurts, but there is a swan pinned to the wall, and somewhere an opinion floating around in someone's jaw is gestating new forms of existence.

Anything can be constructed out of words. A jetty. A kilowatt. Two busy men trying to run a U-Haul station. A leaf dropping slowly through the air.

A trumpet, a smell, a seal. Sea wrack exposed at low tide. A crevice on the border of the real. Trifles light as air. A fury stamped in words.

Skate, skin, skirt. A cathedral of ice.

Ice

There is divinity in ice. Division, incision, and folly on ice. Pleasure on ice. Fish and penguins. Supposition and cubes. Pop. Havoc and wind and North Dakota. Ice on the road. Ice in the west. Ice near the coast where it buttons the cuffs of the moon. Such is the nature of ice. I like ice. Ice on a river. Ice on a lake. Ice when it goes in a glass. Ice coming apart in a river. Ice floating away in chunks. Ice dropping from a glacier and crashing into the sea. This is ice. Diamonds and phases. Facets and phrases. This is a paragraph of ice. Hardened words. Words frozen together. Words frozen temporarily together. For if they melt in your mind the ice is undone. The ice is undone in drips. The ice is undone in chips. The ice is undone in chunks and cubes. Slivers and rivers. Trickles and drops. Otherwise it is words. It is just words. It is not ice it is words. Words resembling glass. Words meaning glass. Only you can decide. Only you can decide what is glass and what is not glass. The fact of these words is ice. A fact is a pulse wrapped in tinfoil. I mean to be exact. I mean to use emphasis. I mean to be transparent. I mean to be translucent. I mean to bring words together in a manner that is satisfactory to us both. I mean to wedge some ice between these words and let it melt into meaning. Meaning thaw. Meaning wet. Meaning cubes. Meaning ice. Incisive ice. Nice and concise. Ice.

A Pamphlet of Snow

A pamphlet of snow is the marvelous tinkling that smashes a feeling into tin. There is a piece of solstice showing through. Then telling a story is the way to give all the rest of the description of postage a little muscle and escalation so that it twinkles with the idea of octaves. I did enjoy the magnetism. Magnetism is to novelty what novels are to snowshoes. Magnetism in a novel means existence tastes like welcome. Life is not always unpleasant. Sometimes it is stout. Piccolos are strange. They have heat and light. They rain underwater. They enchant the senses with scale. Extension and paradox. A paradox is when someone is aggressively peaceful or peacefully aggressive or sharp as a piccolo among woodwinds when the violins permeate the air with delicacy. Delicacy is savage with tenderness. Verbs are excited by tense. Tense and delicacy bond to make palaver. Palaver is a compound of speech and friction. Is this paragraph going anywhere? Is it awakening a sense of sunburn? Is skin a form of sheath? What might a word contain that is not already a form of membrane? Here then is a pamphlet of snow that melts and blossoms into momentum. A remarkable momentum is the one that shows that a beach is the same as resistance. Meaning sand and actors. The end is outlined. The beginning is reciprocal. The actuality of dark is detailed later in rhinestone. The weight of a thought is measured in lips and extravagance. The weight of a thought pulls the stars into music. The weight of a thought is proportional to the varnish of fairyland. The weight of a thought is written in a pamphlet of snow.

Laundry

When I do laundry, I like to begin with the soap. I like to lift the cardboard lid of the box of laundry soap, take the plastic dipper, and scrape out the soap. The soap requires scraping because our apartment, which is partly subterranean, with the living room window flush with a garden of ferns and begonias, is extremely high in humidity. The soap cakes together. I like breaking the chunks with the dipper. It is a satisfying action. I fill the dipper with white powdery soap and carry it into the laundry room which is equipped with one washer and one dryer. We share the equipment with three other apartments. Eight people altogether. Eight people and all the clothes they wear, towels they use to dry themselves, bed sheets and pillowcases. It is annoying to find someone else's clothes in the washer. I don't like to handle someone else's clothes. Even when they are soaking wet and compacted and twisted together from being furiously spun during the rinse cycle, they have a very personal feel to them. There is a vague, completely irrational sense of violation. So it is a joy to find the drum of the washing machine empty. I sprinkle the soap on the bottom. The grains make a powdery, granular sound as they hit the metal. There is a slight echo to it.

I return to our apartment for the basket of clothes. The basket is plastic and yellow with the manufacturer's label still stuck to the bottom, Roughneck Laundry Basket, with the picture of a solid, muscular man in a T-shirt and dark wool cap with his arms crossed and a look of tough defiance. He could be a longshoreman, or bos'n on a tug.

I bring the clothes into the laundry room and carefully distribute them around the agitator. That's what it's called: an agitator. Perfect name. Perfect correspondence of word and function.

I distribute the clothes evenly so that the load will be balanced when the washer gets going, churning, spinning, rinsing, huffing, puffing, gurgling, burbling.

When the washer is finished I wrestle the clothes from the drum of the washer and toss them into the dryer. I close the door of the dryer, press the button, and leave. The whirr of the dryer is a soothing sonata of completion. I set the timer for 45 minutes to an hour. When the time is up, I return for the clothes. I arrive in time to feel the heat of them. It is a pleasurable sensation. A feeling of renewal. I bring the basket into the bedroom, dump the clothes on the bed, and begin to fold them. Folding is tedious, but agreeable in its tedium, because it is methodical, systematic, correct. Fold upon fold, sleeve upon sleeve, chaos is stacked in a drawer.

Bubble

A bubble rises to the surface of a piece of paper. There is no water on the paper. The paper is dry. The bubble is an imaginary bubble. It is, therefore, a perfect bubble. A bubble whose essence is purely imaginative. A purely imagined bubble. The word 'bubble' and the bubble itself. If a bubble takes form in your mind it is because the word 'bubble' contains the bubble. Not an actual bubble. But a purely imagined bubble. At the interior of the bubble is nothing but air. Just as there is nothing but air shaping and propelling the word 'bubble.' On the outside of the bubble is the world. The world in its entirety. Which is another form of bubble. Because the world is round and floats in space. The world is a bubble floating in space. But this is a metaphor, a diversion from the actual bubble, the primordial bubble, the bubble I first proposed. The bubble I launched at the outset of this piece. This piece of writing. Which is another species of bubble. A body of air surrounded by a thin membrane of amniotic proposal. A purely imagined bubble. This bubble. This rage for things purely imagined. Imagined qualities as opposed to actual qualities. Non-quantifiable phenomenon. The difference between the real and the imagined. Which may turn out to be not so purely different. These words are surrounded by thought. This bubble of thought. The word bubble and the thought of which it is composed. The word itself and the thing to which it refers. A musical note and the sound of the note. A lake and the water of which the lake is composed. A lake and the fish in the lake. A lake and the life of the lake. Some of which occurs on the surface and some of which occurs below the surface. In brief, a bubble. A round occurrence of swirling liquid. This. This bauble. This bubble. This bell of oblivion. This circle. This animated form. This sphere. This marvelous air of pure possibility. Floating. Floating out of my mouth. Swirling. Popping. Gone.

Fumarole

Crannies spit steam. A patio other than jumping. The rescue of Miles Davis is never red or pink but always a solid extraterrestrial blue. It seems so thermostat that a physics could turquoise familiarity. Rushing around is soon mineralized to coins like the pattern of hair. All the appetite is library and eucalyptus. I recognize England by its constellations of balm. The flutter of gray in a drugstore where aluminum seems stamped. All the sudden bouillon compressed into daisy surf. Cellos and Jupiter are fluid values. Television is a truck, a horizon packed in a cardboard box. As a residence goes up the smitten jugular of time the feeling of imponderability just thuds to the floor. We are natives because our neighbors quiver like mathematics. Writing a sudden nut is pure velocity. Bauxite on television. A carillon of words orchestrating fish. Reptile rainbow with the resistance of a crosswalk. Night is a river the falsetto sings. Equation note. A ravenous humanity sporting apocalyptic insignia. A tomato all map curbed through a linear accelerator. Meaning released in a collapse of floss. A hot kite many quiet flexible people let go into absorption. The ambassador of conformity has decided to rebel against the hem of his weather. The other feather is basted in gypsum. A crinkle soon curved into arms. The salary of a legato evokes pennies of snow. Rain participates in its own moisture. Knock on the elevator when the hydrant dries. The television viola de gamba is better as a sample than a flake of canvas. Visually it is permeated by rattling toast. A chemical is better when it rages in tone like an alibi. Values are the detergent such huddles create on the field when the score is unwelcome. No rich to vistas of Shakespeare. Values are that which fan the cerebral lake to February and fumaroles crack the syllables into phosphor.

The Core of the Problem

Anyone and everyone living knows that living is a problem. Where to find food. Where to find shelter. Where to find leather and coffee and comfort in extremes of weather. Where to find wire. How to build fire. When to dish up the eggs. When to boil them. When to fry them. When to scramble them. Where to find an underlying purpose for all these things. All this fuss. All this bother. This evidence of silver in the smell of rain.

What is needed is twill. What is wanted is wool. Rapture and light from a pen. A carillon of overtones in Nova Scotia. Sunrise folded into Rawalpindi. A stop to the recoil of field artillery.

Radar is to meaning what muscle is to cartilage. The gristle of thought in a mouth full of rags. The candy of obliquity shining wildly in its sugar.

The mind is a movie of luminous fish.

A fold is a charm. There should be an academy of burlap. Schools devoted to burlap. Philosophies devoted to burlap. The smell of burlap. The expedience of burlap. The experience of burlap. The durability of burlap. Burlap in barns. Burlap on cranes. Burlap at construction sites. Burlap everywhere particular and rough.

I owe a debt to superfluity. A language accelerated by the intricacy of traffic. There is a crosswalk on page 54 that is able to control the flight of a football by joining its mass to an aerodynamic glance. If you hurry to page 58 you can catch it. But it will have changed into an ambulance.

The proper study of meringue is meringue. The taste of meringue. The meaning of meringue. The sound of meringue.

Meringue is dulcet in the aural meatus. It is like the use of sfumato in painting, a folding of tone. Tone upon tone like tongue upon tongue.

Anything sharp and specific or green and perpetual. Anything iron, or framed in pearls. The silence of virtue. The swoop of engagement. A kitchen drawer filled with the reverie of stars.

What We Are What Are We

Yesterday I hung "The Sadness of the King" on the wall with two nails and two picture hangers. The atmosphere in the room changed instantly. My mood turned rapid and tall, like an escalator kicking up sparks from a fire. Epiphany burning in a truth palpable as scissors. Pieces of colored paper. An old man's hands cutting a genie out of gouache. Mettle in red, wisdom in green, composure in blue. Equations of sunlight and glue.

It is reassuring and sweet to believe space is curved. Yesterday's sandwich is not today's sandwich. A perfect sandwich cannot be assembled out of cold cuts and pumpernickel. The distinction between the beautiful and the ugly has a social aspect. We all occupy different rooms. Patterns, corollaries, categories. Insights kindled with nuance.

The world is a bucket of possibility crackling with cause and effect. Hence, poetry. Language mangled into collarbones. Windows speckled with rain. Mica poking out of a wallet full of identity and age.

There is nothing more baroque than human reproduction. Later, there is a dilation of anger and bone. Writing heaves with instincts. A shadow broken from its eyes and sifted through the debris of a necktie.

Television refrigerates children. One should give them an ethics of action and involvement. Luggage in intricate stars. Crickets immersed in music. A dagger of light draped in black velvet.

The waves come in slowly at first, surge into waves that are grasped with furious paddling. It is the most elusive thing in one's existence. A red Pontiac with a dream-catcher hanging from the rear-view mirror making a left into a cemetery.

A bruise. A weave. A cat in the kitchen window.

Thracian helmet in a funeral home.
A flurry of blossom on Bigelow.
An old man looking for an address.

Gray's Anatomy

It's hard to like gray. It is inherently mournful. It smacks of death and prophecy and Macbeth. It lingers in the air like a raw uncertainty. It floats like an immense contusion above the earth, the residue of a collision between white and black, good and evil, being and nothingness. Gray is the color of thought. Thought is gray because it emanates from the brain and the brain the human brain is gray. Gray as a cloud when it is tinged with thunder. Gray as a cloud when it is tinctured with bulk. Borders and definitions collapse in gray. Borders and definitions collapse in thought. This is what makes thought gray. Ambiguity. Ambiguity makes the color of thought gray. And clouds and ashes and compromise and accommodation gray. Everything uncertain and indistinct and equivocal is gray. But this isn't always the case. Things get sticky here. It is the nature of gray to get sticky. And confused. Because battleships and destroyers and sidewalks are gray. And battleships and destroyers and sidewalks are brutally gray. Are brutally certain and distinct. So you see what happens when one enters the realm of gray. Nothing sticks. And everything sticks. Because gray inclines toward tenuity and dissolution. But it is also the color of cannons and resolution. It is the color of phantoms and tombstones and Edgar Allan Poe. But it is also the color of the USS Hornet USS Missouri USS Shenandoah and the USS Seattle. It is also the color of the sidewalk on McGraw the sidewalk on Fifth Avenue North the sidewalk on Roy the sidewalk on Ray and the sidewalk on Phinney Avenue North. Some sidewalks veer toward off-white but the older sidewalks are incontrovertibly gray. Gray is the color of cemetery mists and glacial terrains. But it also has an urban dimension. Because in sidewalks

and parking lots and building foundations the permeability and oatmeal-
-like quality of cement hardens into a hue of gray so emphatic in its
grayness it forgives all inattention with the grace of its anonymity.
Because gray is the sorcery of transition. Because gray is the arithmetic
of smoke. It anoints indecision with the vermouth of nuance. It blesses
definition with the gauze of ambiguity. The cello employs gray in the
resonance of its base. There is gray in excursion and gray in
horticulture. Gray is the mood of northern Europe steeped in its books.
Like a painting by Breughel. Like a mist moving through the forests of
Bavaria. Gray is the color of the world on the first morning of its
existence. Gray is the color of existence. Existence when it is gray.
Existence when it has everything and nothing to say.

Starlings

Starlings annoy me. I cannot say why. Partly, it has to do with their numbers. Their murmurations, as they are called. They swarm, teem, hunt and peck everywhere with great aggression. Their speckled, greenish-purple bodies have a gloss that gives them the appearance of being greased. Greased for aggression. They drive out bluebirds and woodpeckers. They carouse in the millions. A murmuration of starlings will eat 20 tons of potatoes and foul what they leave behind. They spread histoplasmosis (a disease of the lungs similar to tuberculosis caused by a fungus), gastroenteritis virus, and cherry blossom brown rot. In 1960 a Lockheed Electra stirred up 10,000 starlings as it left Boston's airport. The plane went straight into the tumultuous murmuration. It engines strangled on the starlings and 62 people died. Crews from the Oregon Department of Transportation once spent an hour firing a propane-powered orchard cannon on the southbound span of the Interstate 5 bridge over the Columbia river between Vancouver and Portland in an effort to persuade the murmuration to murmur elsewhere. Did it work? I cannot say.

Compared to crashed planes and lung disease, my complaints are frivolous. My health and well-being have not been compromised by rampant murmurations. Starlings are common. But so are pigeons, seagulls, sparrows, robins, and crows. I am indifferent to pigeons, entertained by the swoop and glide of seagulls, diverted by the quickness and buffoonery of sparrows, regaled by the chirp of robins, and fond of crows. I enjoy all these birds. It is not a matter of number.

My complaint with starlings has to do with something else. I believe it is their ill-humor. Starlings are grouchy. Humorless.

Everything they do they do in a spirit of propagation. But propagation to no purpose other than propagation. Propagation for the purpose of propagation. Humorless, rigorous, Spartan reproduction.

And I find this spirit of diligent reproduction deeply ironic, considering the fact the starling is not a native bird. They were introduced to the United States in 1890 by a drug manufacturer named Eugene Scheiffelin who decided that New York should be home to all of Shakespeare's songbirds. It is hard to think of a starling as a songbird, much less a creature of one of Shakespeare's plays. It strikes me as a situation where the word exceeds the dullness of its reality.

Starling is a pretty word. Murmuration is a pretty word. The starling, in its speckled, greenish-purple reality, is something more than pretty. It is banal. Pretty but banal. Pretty in its banality. As if something pretty as a pearl or an ingot of gold might suffer a similar fate. How does something intrinsically pretty become banal? Or is the banality in the murmuration of the starling a murmuration that is in me, a capacity for banality that resides under my skin? This, I find, may well be the case. When I find myself sliding into banality I do the natural thing. I do what is most expedient. I bring out a volume of Shakespeare and plunge into it. Immerse my being in it. Immerse my being in its words. Its starlings and storms. Its great huge storms and bright, iridescent birds. Its cobs and pots and mausoleum worms. Its fruits and dishes. Its oceans and words. It isn't long before all those cobs and pots and storms and worms bring about a difference in me. Precisely what, I cannot say. But a starling seems more than a starling, and a savor is more than a taste.

Open House

Let us go into the house. It is a big house. It is larger than an igloo, yet smaller than a violin. Let us become acquainted with its tints. I see a red door and I want to paint it black. No colors anymore I want them to turn black. There are volumes on the walls and fur in the furniture. The wind is outside. It blows around spreading description. Various holes terminate in mud. The plumbing maneuvers water. The plumbing cannot be seen. It is inside the walls. We know it is there because we can hear it gurgle and hiss. It offers faucets and taste. It offers figures and rain. One by one the walls reveal art. This is a Matisse. This is a Picasso. See how the highway becomes a thick endeavor. We must endeavor to endeavor to understand endeavor. All highways endeavor to take us places. Highway 61 goes from Mississippi to Chicago. Meanwhile the house protects us like a fullback. The house wanders through its lines like a cave. The house comforts us and completes a mosaic of cups. There is a balloon inside whose radius is blessed with plywood. Sheetrock provides section and shape. The windows provide songs. The doors provide knobs. We experience the floor as a form of intention. It protects our feet from rocks and opposition. The carpet enhances the sensation of the spine. It beckons us to walk on it. It beckons us to lie on it. It introduces us to beckoning. It introduces us to the weight of our bones and the climate of our skin. Photographs on the walls make life appear hysterical and wicker. The space in the house is fluid. We are bathed in divertimento. Deliveries occur in the vestibule. A subterranean moon implies the garage is a coin of music. But in actuality the garage glides into our perception as an adjunct, or mass. Mass pertains to volume as volume pertains to distribution and this results in a house of language. Videos woo the lure of the fable. Their stories open us to possibilities of sepia. Our bodies are fables of skin and blood. The skull is a house of bone. The brain is a house of nerve. These are metaphors. The metaphor is a house of sticks. Skeletons swarming with Rembrandt. Hefty emotions of light and shadow. Alternating links of phosphate and deoxyribose. If a man dies, shall he live again? And in what house? A chip off the old block. A chip of benefit which benefits from rock. Wonder is a chip of immersion in scope. Abstraction is a house of spheres and charcoal. We all live in a yellow submarine. We all live in a house of language. Our house of being. Our house of non-being. Our house of nothingness and bunting. Our bungalow of bonnyclabber. Our house of Poland. Our house of Greece. Our house of babble. Our house of books. Our white house. Our black house. Our house of jelly and ink.

The New Neighbors

The new neighbors are difficult. They pound on our door at night seeking welcome and pudding. We can only give them trinkets of glass and a little chloroform, for which they are deeply grateful, and leave baskets of jute and asterisks in return.

Who are these people? We listen to them, learn to read their moods using a suite of remote sensing instruments and a vial of African earth. Their sublimely irrelevant décor fills us with trepidation. Strange noises infiltrate the floor as they do whatever it is they do above us, shuffle about, or coordinate a universe of fossil conjunctions and centrifugal grommets. The few suppositions we have drawn from telescope observations indicate knots of anguish tinctured with sodium hydroxide. In a continent of extremes, this sort of thing is to be expected, but their strange pallor and foghorns combine to produce a sense of privation that is difficult to fathom, especially if one considers the magnitude of their pantry, which is full of beans and toothpicks.

They sometimes welcome us in the hallway, bouncing laser beams off the surface of our clothing. For me, this has always been the very essence of perception, these interludes in the hallway, these interludes in time, that afford us transitory glimpses of one another during some of our most unguarded moments, when we are getting the mail, for instance, or poking our head out the door to see what the weather is like.

I have always wanted to see Elvis in person, and they seem to intuit this about me, and know that it will never be possible, since Elvis is dead, dead from exhaustion, dead from the rigors of fame and pharmaceuticals, in the late 70s, when Disco was king. I believe this is why they once left a stack of albums at our door, Blue Hawaii, Kissin' Cousins, Double Trouble, and Clambake.

There is a dailiness that is hard to convey to the outside world, but occasionally one is treated to certain insights in videos starring Ben Affleck or Dustin Hoffman that serve to unite us, that serve to create a sense of domesticity shared with other people however dissimilar their background and tastes. It is this, this daily uniformity I attempted to bring to our neighbors in the form of a photo album gangrenous from humidity, which I believe was central in motivating them to teach me the sounds of their alphabet, enunciations which swiveled and squirmed in my mouth like spasms of brackish colloquy.

After a solid week or so of remodeling they invited us up for a look. Vast, engineered canals extended from their kitchen into the living room. Planets sparkled on the ceiling. Nuclear powered appliances hummed with resolute efficiency.

Have I mentioned the crows? Hundreds of crows hopped about on the chairs and tables. In some of the darker corners, eyes iridesced in exquisite chiaroscuro.

A laboratory full of ceramics and jars overwhelmed the senses with sprawling, penetrating odors. One of them opened a sleepy eye and emitted a low growl of contentment.

On one occasion I brought them a piece of Gorgonzola cheese. The one named Chabouk took a bite, then spit it out, and shook with fury. I apologized, but I did not know why the old fellow had reacted with such vehement anger. This strained our relations.

One night, it was necessary that I knock on our bedroom ceiling with a broom. One of our new neighbor's were fussing about in the kitchen and making a lot of weird noises. This strained our relations even further. I tried to make things better by bringing them a bowl of fudge the next day. This, too, garnered hostility, and the door was slammed in my face.

I returned home and stared out the window, baffled. Out there among the quiet stones I could see the day implicitly defined by parks and pleats of mist. Each passing day churned out some 80,000 images of various lifestyles and clothing. In a world where the clouds can sometimes go from silver to gold in an instant it's important to understand the vicissitudes of existence. All it takes is a little blackjack now and then to remind us how vulnerable we are.

It's hard to avoid people when they happen to live right above you. They would appear sometimes in the hallway gliding down to do their laundry, their strange, membranous wings pulsing in veins big as hawsers, a silvery sheen on their skin faintly glistening. One wondered, in fact, what they needed clothes for in the first place.

Their conversations, which were barely audible through the drinking glass I pressed to the ceiling, provided a fresh new understanding. They were, after all, just as baffled and burdened by the mysteries of existence as we were. Just as the male mandarin fish flares his fins to woo the smaller, egg-filled female, I could hear Chabouk utter things that impregnated the surrounding air with the hydraulics of inquiry, judgments challenged and examined in a dreamy world of unearthly acoustics. Bumping, trembling, sometimes hissing, I could hear their bodies flex and harden as they discussed traditions and attitudes with a view toward mollifying the wounds created by life's thorns. Listening in on their world taught me a great thing. I learned that we are all laboring to build a continent of hope out of nothing but fog and soap.

Their words trembled with splendid colors as if they had ice in them, trampolines and facts. Shadows of heaven lashed by wind and rain.

Over the months we began to grow more intimate. The dazzling displays of wholehearted indifference now began to gurgle with renewed heat. Parrots and omelettes graced our conversation.

Sometimes I would see them return from a casual outing, bounce down the sidewalk on their blue hind legs exhibiting extremes of temperature in their eyes, fighting cold and loneliness with strips of tarpaulin and twists of licorice. Black scrawls etched by Martian dust devils danced on the hull of their ship. The intricate tattoos on their faces lampooned the irrepressible conviviality of pancakes.

I realized that kinship extends far beyond our immediate family, far beyond our species. We are all united by strings, scabs, and hormones. The quest to understanding laces the history of all sentient creatures. The pretty white blossoms of the bloodroot or the winged jewels biology offers us in the form of scarabs all imply a certain naked benevolence underlying all personality, even if it is the mere ejaculatory spasm of a zealous appendage.

I found myself much of the time having to scrape up the white crystals my neighbors left after evaporating. They would sometimes boil, freeze, or poof into vapor if amused by a joke or angered by a dead battery. Chabouk would sometimes burst into a shower of tiny stars at the slightest mention of a Scandinavian smorgasbord. He was curiously aroused by the idea of a smorgasbord. He thought it had something to do with baptising jackknives.

Perfume and cordovan defy common wisdom. This is the way of all sentient behavior. It fusses over things like stationary, sends out birthday cards and wedding invitations, regenerates its life on paper where it assumes the chromatic aberrations of a novel or poem. A metaphor might be forever etched into jade, old men climbing a mountain in China to discover the meaning of existence, and finding a jukebox whose titles include some early songs from the British invasion of the 60s.

Chabouk's favorite song was called "She's Not There," by the Zombies. He said he found it druidical, solitary, and savage, not unlike a swimming pool perched on bedsprings. I told him it reminded me of the warm disposition of velour, roiling ash and rings of steam.

Chabouk had a way of opening his heart I found particularly ingratiating. By that I mean, he could do it literally, reach into his chest cavity and bring out his heart to show us its hidden channels and shorelines. A just palpable, wild and delicate aroma emanated from the organ. It seemed to epitomize the very syntax of life as it throbbed rhythmically in his hand before he reinserted it into his body.

Facts have a way of both revealing and obscuring a reality. Human perspective tends to center on water, on fluidity in general, but Chabouk had a way of seeing the world that telescoped into surprising details. Things like old wheel rims, or the smell of mocha on a certain winter afternoon, or the way an usher will sometimes probe his way with a flashlight in a theatre embodied certain truths that exceeded even the most sophisticated mathematics used to explain compound interest, or how populations develop and interact.

There is something starkly alien about an empty apartment. It was on a Thursday that I went to call on Chabouk. My wife and I had been kept awake by the mating calls of frogs. Foam-nest frogs, water lily frogs, and banded rubber frogs. Snoring puddle frogs and tremelo sand frogs. To this was added the cacophony of birds. Thousands of birds. Golden-rumped tinker barbets, Burchell's coucals, Klass's cuckoos, spotted dikkops, purple-crested louries, and tambourine doves. I could identify these sounds since I had once been a Miami hairdresser. The shampoos we used tended to draw wildlife, rhinos and rogue dishevelments seeking mirrors and conformity. It was high time I had a discussion with Chabouk about his family's nocturnal activities, and the 200 or so Greco-Roman mummies left in the laundry room.

I knocked at the door for a considerable length of time. I knew someone was home because I could hear subatomic particles continually being created and annihilated. On my 712th knock, I discovered the door was unlocked. I twisted the knob and the door opened. I walked into a completely empty apartment. Empty, that is, save for the gravel pit, ceremonial maces, and dozens of little painted ceramic dogs.

Three months later a postcard appeared in our mailbox. It was from Madagascar. The picture on the front featured the Betsimisaraka Music Band. All it said on the back was "Another jarring turn in the data," and was signed Chabouk.

What data? I could not stop thinking about the Persian army at the battle of Marathon, a call to prayer from a nearby mosque, great sails against the sky, this newfound confidence in the possibilities of being mortal, the high-pitched pulsating song of cicadas.

There is always something that flows or flees, that escapes binary organizations, the resonance apparatus, and the overcoding machine: things that are attributed to a "change in values," or the micropolitics of a condominium building. Ever attend a condo meeting? It is there we learn the true nature of pitch. The value of a feeling is sometimes determined by syncopation.

They say an elevator fattens on generalities. What else can you say in an elevator? You're either going up or going down. It is you who chooses which floor to visit, but the cables and pulleys remain the same. Sometimes moving to a new domain brings us into contact with ourselves. That it is to say, our forgotten, neglected selves. As if the spectacular backdrop of our lives were not the tropical scenes we had imagined but a large body of water propelled by cello through a room painted off-white with an accent wall in pale green.

Opinions are the tools of conversation. If I'm looking at a full moon, a new moon, or just a sliver, is everyone around the world seeing the same phase I am? Does the Statue of Liberty wear shoes? When do wildebeests migrate through the Serengeti?

Ancient Greeks thought our eyes acted as lanterns, sending out rays that made objects visible when struck. One tends to value any kind of statement for what one can take from it as a link, or photoelectric cell. Such a way of speaking will have, of course, an immediate impact on those with whom we share a common space, and it will either be one of respect and sympathy, or a questioning of the kind of data they present to us, and we present to them. If they disturb us during dinner with their constant pounding, pounding that they promised would not occur, because their floorboards would dovetail together gently, requiring only glue, then it is up to us to decide whether this was a ruse to trick us into compliance, or a sop intended to absorb our editorializing, and render it neutral by their seeming indifference.

It was a happy thought to build the Hudson river railroad right along the shore. We live on the edge of a deep, deep pointlessness, which is to say nothing original, nothing effortful or fresh, but said simply to fill a space, a space left empty by exhumation, memories dug out of the head, and committed to paper. All it takes is a fresh new set of eyes to set everything in motion again.

Meanwhile, a new set of neighbors have moved in with a new set of annoyances to battle, or transcend: enigmatic rites, colossal collisions, steam blasts, drifting plates, aggressive copulation, bounding impala, laundry left in the washing machine. Pride, retribution, regret. The stuff of existence. The grammar of proximity, savage and acrobatic in its critical mass.

The Serendipity of Seeds

What is the best way to experience space? Space travel is one tack. Another is to taste it. Taste it how? By immersing it in your mind and mulling it over. Pack it in a suitcase. Wear it to a wrestling match. Play it on a lute. Bottle it. Burn incense in it. Smash it against a wall. You will begin to notice that the space between an orange and a volume of Shakespeare has a taste similar to the fog when it is folded into words for dramatizing the opacity of pearls. The space in a rattlesnake is pulled by the arithmetic of crawling. Architecture is the celebration of space in vaults and tracery. Columns, flutes, and halls. Porticos, cotillions, and balls. When space is painted in Spanish it is arranged in poplars and cork. Beards are distinguished by the activity of squirrels. Squirrels are more precise than clocks because they live in trees and amuse the dirt. This is why the space between trees is so crucial to the serendipity of seeds. The splendor of space is blue and black. It is blue in the air, black on a hat. Ribbon expands the capacity to understand space as a deformity, or hippodrome for negotiating gravity. Otherwise, it hangs from the sky like a curtain of green and gold, or pullulates with stars on a river moving perfectly by itself.

Philip Lives: A Lament for Lamantia

Philip is gone. Philip is dead. Long live Philip.

Philip lived and breathed poetry. He called poetry a miracle in words. Which is precisely what it is. A miracle in words. Rhapsodes of pain passionate wavelengths tortured minerals sublimated into bubbling autonomy. Delicious anomalies paradisiacal pancakes morning prayer in the bowl of dawn. Fireworks in Mexican villages. The aroma of dragons. Analogues parallels pantisocratic parakeets.

Piles of sawdust on the workshop floor. An errant chorus in a stick of sequence. Fragments of meaning utopian as towels and metaphysical as a sheepskin rug.

If anyone refers to this as word play I will punch them in the nose. Surrealism is not word play surrealism is a mouthful of light a towering urge to mangle the language beat it into tungsten a raging river fastened to the hood of a jeep old clocks yawning in oysters oracular ore at the core of an oar a Martian umbrella dressed in music.

Philip was a regular at the eternal smorgasbord of mood and penumbra. He astonished us all with his granite balloons his sensations and hurry his addiction to talking his elevators and hardware his opinions and theories his immense curiosity his ceaseless thermos of romantic green tea. His beads his buds his beans his occasional beards.

A lament is sad but this isn't sad this is a black emotion pinned to a crimson grammar this is a feeling in the form of a needle a basketball of glass a thought made of ribbon a jar of headlights a Tuesday varnished with sonnet milk the smell of popcorn in a theatre lobby the month of July split open to reveal topaz trout swimming in a sewing box a city of toads and charming absorptions desperado poets beating on a gong a phantom hammerhead walking around in its previous bones.

He reminded me a little of Peter Lorre he could talk for hours emitting a reddish glow of crocodiles and ethereal escalators a poetry of X rays and telepathic plumage a piece of weather reflected in the sheen of ocean sand fairyland teeming with diamonds the convulsive variety of curbs in Pakistan the anatomy of any flavor sunspots radio waves crackling the rumble of palominos on Colorado dirt.

He would enter a state of rapture and tell you poetry is not a palliative but a provocation. That we live in a subterranean homesick world. That the beauty of a rattlesnake is an astonishing thing. That the rattle of the rattlesnake shows philosophy and taste.

One afternoon he got tangled in the seatbelt of our Subaru and kept right on talking vivid as a medieval illumination struggling to get out of the material world.

He had a fever for the marvelous for photosynthesis and caves for Matisse for Magritte for a can of cantatas. For the Dada jackpot of a chemical railroad sizzling in a cast iron frying pan. For banjos and balusters and bandaged horizons nostalgic as nudes for syllables for solder and jackknives for acetylene sardines liquid oxygen seasoned with thyme for a woman's gaze drowning in gauze for being and nothingness infinity plunged in clouds a camel squeezed through the eye of a needle Rimbaud walking the streets of Harar the quality of light in a stained glass window a silver watch hemorrhaging mohair the immensely deliciously ineffable thrill of saying the unsayable without being able to say it. For bookstores embroidered with alleys for the pathology of crosswalks for knowledge coined in the halls of cranberry for torque for torsion for incidental light for the Big Bang exploding out of Mallarme's fan for the mocha machinery of eighteenth century Ecuador for the guts of a word stuck in somebody's ear for wool for outmaneuvering burlap for unpacking a suitcase of swords and kettledrums and smokestack lightning.

Dear Philip thank you for the legacy. For the consonants orbiting a vowel. For the axles and gears of magnetic tiaras greased by incantation. For the extraordinary ordinariness of a wheelbarrow burdened with the lung of a Sumerian pronoun. For the elevator paneled with insect wings. For the batch of words baked in eucalyptus and polished with Deadwood, South Dakota. For the hypodermic feeling of a resplendent opinion pinned to my lip. For writing wild and writing a wilderness. For a sense of history swimming with music. For teaching me that poetry is necessary and cruel because it is the first thing in the world to come alive. For being alive. For thrusting your tongue into a pubis of loam and telling us what it tasted like. For the many prepositions surgically removed from a jukebox. For your hat of shoals and Shasta pollen. For your crystal rails and volcanic sunsets.

What apparel best suits these sentiments? How shall I dress to say a final farewell to you?

Words with shiny black exoskeletons and watercolor birds. A gem with a head. A life on the brink. Geometric odors flaring in the siroccos of my unmitigated hat.

Phantom Jam

As diffusion is pressed into thought the prunes go bald as baritones. The clay has since found its skin, and begins to move toward neon, expecting thread. What lovely grain swills the sunlight today. The foible of the nest is proven in the whirling of the puddle. Even the crustaceans blossom toward a newer luminescence, a type of leather unique to the evolution of glass. The asterisks, grown heavy, crumple into fiction. Justice has grown flabby, but the radiation of meat is too mannered to police as mathematics. Hence, the enzymes do us proud creating muscle, hormones, and cuffs. All be curb, all be calm in the zoo cafeteria. I can be real catty sometimes, like when the zither rolled its gout down the street, its wheels jiggling like the wheels on grocery carts, and I called the grant panel a complex lower plant. What ghosts we saw. How we pined for the asphalt. Our coats shifting slippery on our backbone, we entered the wax museum at twilight, the sun spreading its fire across the bay. The glass there was honest as distillation's goulash. We move toward wool conscious of bamboo, thinking stomachs and napkins are linked to dinner in a way far more natural than we initially dreamed. The napkins turned soggy in the sauna, but the kilowatts were real, and the squirrels thought death all the way up the tree. Where is the blood inside a word? Certain parts mean Shakespeare consciously, as death accelerates the landscape into sudden dread, bundles of breathing and bugs. Art's intensity is one part pitch, one part scent. Bulge for rhythm. The metamorphosis of gray is receiving ablution. The scaffold is charged with the whole of the burden, an eyeball absorbing the vision of change as an insurgent bell yells proximity to a leviathan integrity of winter. Time is partly vibrant in this season of snow and candy. What the cellar doesn't bog with sunflowers the heather infuses with grace. Hence, the alley turns comic with its own dripping and the coffee burns along the lapel. There is yet an oyster or two to describe the scab of day. An ethereal froth rides the thought of a proud idea, an easy tense wrapped in the temperament of a long crusade for aesthetic fluorescence. The maple lake crunches underfoot. The diplomat is speaking German. The propeller is shaping up. It has a nice woody odor. Or would it be better to say smell? What is the difference between an odor and a smell? How fat the abstraction of it seems, a blatant attempt to confound the ambiguity of fragrance with the keen sensation of reaching into the hollow of a freshly carved pumpkin. There is a greenhouse feeling attached to this search for an earthy abstraction, as if satellites weren't enough, and what was needed was a reddish-brown landscape, a feeling that the cosmos is immanent as spit.

Martha Marmalade

Thought is a cupola of rumination for the fortitude of knickknacks. A paragraph is acorns. All through insisting on heaven a cantata cheers a spring of hammers. Reality is astounding. Heaven is a place that papers the bruise of existence with space. This is the cue for Martha. Martha Marquisette. Martha Marmalade. Martha Charity. Martha painting an estuary. Martha going to New Mexico with a spectrum of stains. This makes everything a narrative. This makes everything a morning of passion and being. Such suddenly teeming ideas white episodes of muscle front the udder as it hangs. A fact draped over a branch whose fever is a nimble rhyme transparent as time. Thought rhymes with dot a sentence somersaulting over the debris of its own data. Balance is grace. An aerosol assuming the balance of air whereas a film happens by spinning itself into motion and weather. Bell the Amazon dangle a bayou among boots. Propeller fountain trembling as do neckties about to knot themselves into density. Nor fluid nor insect may wedge damask to diamond as along this bristle of sound. A wrinkled man writing poetry on Saturday. Eggs are the anatomy you chafe against time. Meaning is produced by implication. Nylon snags a sonnet. Much ado about cameras some of which capture the aroma of fable. It is the debut of the universe. Cedar amplifies the amenity of daybreak. A drop of fire is later than you fiddle and is soon a form of language. For when day is broken it becomes a harmonica spewing blues. Martha Propagation. Martha Glamour. Coffee ethereal with black.

Ajar in Tennessee

I placed a jar in Tennessee and it sprawled around like an unguent. This is the kind of medicament that objectifies passage. If there is a rodeo on the radio we recommend ribs. By we I mean me. I said that to mean I am very daring. Why don't I say eucalyptus then. Eucalyptus then. Let us all say eucalyptus. Stretches and stretches of eucalyptus. I placed a jar in Tennessee and it exploded into eucalyptus. This gives the nearby aluminum a mandate. Henry James said it was a complex thing to be an American and now I know why. There is a fire in all of us that opposes the tyranny of routine. Aluminum is available in many wrought forms such as tubing, extruded shapes, sheet and bar, and is widely used to make everything from radiators to pistons to intake manifolds. An alloy is allowed to alliterate intellect for emphasis. Here is another fact. Aluminum is approximately 1/3 the weight of steel, yet some aluminum alloys exhibit tensile strengths greater than some low carbon steels. This is easy to say because pelicans stand in external existence tied to an external world. Contemplation enjoys freedom, and while the necessity of nature shows a complete disregard for banks, the words move back and forth on pulleys depicting boulders purged of subjective opinion. The burden of the incommunicable occurs in large twisting, branching masses. Because such a thing is, it is, and as it is, so it ought to be. You may one day star in a superb musicalization of Anna and the King of Siam. You may wonder why inward and outward are empty forms. Control your bathrobe. It is the customary mistake of reflection to take the essence to be merely the interior. We like linen and balloons as well. But why paleontology? Why this fixation on fossils, and rock? Because there is a man in each woman and a woman in each man. So dig. Dig my friend. Look inside and tell me what you see. Is it a casino? Not everything is buckskin. Some things burn with an inner light. Like a brick. Like a rock. Like a jar on a hill in Tennessee.

Native Emulsion

The sad history of neon awaits me at the end of the hall. How will I get there? How will I pattern the bronze? Any hand propelled by airplane is much too parliamentary to participate in paper. True expression requires an affectionate jump. Imaginary grievances have always been more my torment than real ones. A human being is an animal soaked in personality. It takes a cold and hard mathematical formula to emulsify a mood. It occurs to me that a wedding is all surf and thrill. The first time I was ever invisible I operated a temperature called hurry. We have but one rose to pledge to opinion. I cannot help thinking Mr. Audubon a dishonest man. A fine note snagged on a sundae and proffered to us all as a baritone. In our world of perpendicular walls and floors it is the blade itself that matters as the newlyweds recoil. Life is never entirely intestinal. It is also a tissue of rain, fountains, and fire. Everything else is either metallic, or plywood. Whenever I find myself growing vaporish, I rouse myself, wash and put on a clean shirt, brush my hair and clothes, tie my shoestrings neatly, and go out into the world to add another chapter to my autobiography. Time is but a jackknife between mayhem and rhapsody. The 16th century was cauterized by flippers. Yesterday I languished in silk. Today I crush the minutes under the hooves of my reindeer. Now I am going to enter on the subject of self, which is a spectrum in gusts and giddy as a waterfall. Its miraculous transformations fatten on values which are largely pardonable, and cockeyed. A muscle inflates the daybreak of the hand. Pelicans squabble on the sand. In the midst of the world I live like a hermit. I have conversations with Peru. My occupation is entirely literary. A cerebral sparrow ornaments the hood of my jeep. The angle of incidence equals the angle of reflection. I better understand the pragmatism of skin with that thing they call a name. I am not in the least judge of the proper weight and size of an infant. But I do know how to name it. The slow wheels of time permit a sense of linearity to seek consummation in curbs and percussion. This very habit would be parent of idleness and difficulties were it not also delicately sprinkled into a silver vial, covered with spirits, and ignited. A fable is born. The penumbral chain is all glaze and piccolo. Tables with false tops, trap doors, thin wires or threads transform the rodeo. For the first time anything seems possible. Becoming someone else, for instance, or the ability to walk through a wall. The laboratory of invention is an affable adobe. Mirrors are practically useless to me. Chopin turns the air blue. A resplendent spittle hurts the time into licorice. The great beauty of poetry is that it makes everything algebra. A body of air twisted into fish.

Better Homes and Abstractions

My wife and I want to move but we cannot agree on the sort of place we'd like to inhabit. I want to live in a laboratory for testing ottomans. She wants to live in a jukebox full of long corridors and stratospheric counterpoints. I want to live in a limestone cantata in Anchorage, Alaska. She wants to live in a blade of grass with thirty-two rooms and a washcloth made of moonlight. I want to live in a climate of words whose clumsiness is supple as a minuet. She wants to live in a logarithm carpeted with magnolia petals. She insists that her logarithm be constructed of the finest irrational numbers available and that all the windows are orthogonal polynomials and all the doors are alluring solutions to space and time. Our realtor is frustrated, but stimulated by our many requirements. She shows us house after house after house. Each time we stomp on the floor to check for grammar and syntax. The house of language is not a box with a roof on it but a mansion of many appliances. Syllables, sensations, plumbing. "I want to live in a texture," my wife insists. "What kind of texture," I ask. "Any texture," she replies. "All textures." I assure her that the house of language is a text of infinite texture. But my wife is more mathematically inclined than I. She worries about the geometry. "What about shape," she asks. "What about depth and volume? What about length and width? What about fortitude and shirts?" The house of language has all these things. The house of language is built of thought, which is a lumber like pine, with knots and resin. Which is a species of reason. Which is an adventure of corners and knobs. Which is a suite of assertions. Which is a tabernacle of words. Which is a protective shell. Which is a tegument or rind. Which is a melon. Which is a thing put forward on a vine. Which is a ramification. Which is an eidolon, a fruit that ripens in the mind. "But the mind must have a head," asserts my wife, "and a skull to keep it dry." And this is true. But not so true it pleads concrete. Or the testament of form. It is more like a dirigible, or balloon. Something that rises, then drifts through the sky.

Ceremony of Wings

$\mathcal{S}$ay it say it now as I feel it the warm summer air outside the jumble of emotion inside. The machinery of doubt. Blemish of apprehension. Seesaws of sophistry nimble equivocation pleasant sensations of scale indulged in uproar pearls scabs Muddy Waters it is all a matter of cogs flaps spouts. The sputter of increase murmur of inspiration. Fumes from a fissure in the earth. I say them as I feel them smell them taste them crash them hew them curl them into words knots freight package them into pronouns prospects personalities. Gauze of thought. Sunken treasure. Twists of air amber and rose. Refraction. Reflection. Dots. My life in words in arcs in spectrums of locomotive salt. Regrets whispers lies. Things that bother me things that please me unnecessary things things that cry for necessity things that hardly seem things at all they are so nebulous so ravenous for form they assume the folly and molecular cogency of a rake. I saw one, once, leaning against a wall in a garage. It spoke to me of long use and durability. Not literally, of course, but with its prongs, its tenable externality. Hardness, unassimilability, bur. The formal category of resistance. Resistance to what? The pliability of the sponge. The languor of absorption. The rake is awake. Awake in its wood as would a cord in accordance play length for a sauce. Vast tracts of time waxy and veined. Fat radiant depths suggest a kind of dock, or emotion. Emotion annealed in ink. Where it is possible to match a feeling to an image. A play of light. A moon. An eagle in a spiral of calm. Water crashing, thunderously, into a basin of stone. Sky crazed with lightning. Rain on aluminum broken into summer. Imagine it how you will. Your life. My life. My life in your life. Your life in my life. His life. Her life. Their life. Roles we play.

Fangs bared. Tongues loosened. Favors performed. Old oils maroon lemon opera pink in gobbets and specks on a palette. An object it is good to feel, something warm and pulsing or cold and brass. Something dripping. Something immediate and present. Not like time but buttons on a jukebox. A yolk of pain in a glair of sound. Bits of broken shell. A song in the shape of a leaf. Beak. Ceremony of wings.

The Conservation of Strangeness

It is keen and convincing to quiver a who. The pronoun stands in rage to a nickel stool. Daubed with pessimism, she never smirked at the extrusion of words these kind of biceps dream. It is longer to crinkle among the wells. A palette of penicillin might be imagined as an aerosol, or hotel. Did alpaca ignite reverie England would dream its fifths? The night gets crowded behind the gateway barrel. A sudden horse naked as that debris we call a rhythm emits deep penumbral agreements of almond alliteration. With smatterings of sound up and down the upholstery of the sonnet, we find a pallet is required to whistle the ribs. Humanism is impolitic as a marathon is thick with effort. Sunglasses make it so the phosphor is better humanized by foam than balsa. We did with the downs what the monarchs do with their parts in Shakespeare. That is to say dinner opens the back of the passport and bathes it in sticks. That spacecraft we saw the other night is now smoldering unanimously among the embroidered thuds of chattered color. I twisted the aria with a crowbar long before I noticed the adze. It sometimes happens in an airport that an extraordinary sentence will evolve into a play outside the parameter of flags decorating the plaza. Thelonious Monk once played the piano like that. He leaned forward into the carpentry of sounds so inflamed with music they caused knots of cognition to unravel into sail. This is why the railroad oak has the sudden trestle of a pet. Versailles thrives in such films and lifts the light as a circumference penned by fins. Delicate wants lie near the trout repaired in evaporation like a towel. The translucent nod we sometimes find in a bagel, or a wattle greased with thermal fat. The stepladder is companionable, a back window full of astronomy. Nothing to get upset about. Any insect is more allegorical than the most ebullient rainbow California saw inflate with helium light. Words are not enough and more than enough. This is why Vermeer could do with no other constellations than curtain, milk, and pail.

Today is for Detail

I was about to nail the harmonica reservoir to my necktie when I realized life is a palate soon scripted by a thermometer. I was one waterfall shy of a baluster requisition. It is not invisible to perpetuate a sample of this. Sweat is dry when it solves absence. These words, for instance, represent screams, limestone giggles ridged with administration. It isn't deep to yawn at dinner. Leaves resemble thread in spacecraft even. Diamonds are less chromatic than amethyst but writing surrounds them with ginger. A living struggling rescue of peas. A keen rotation of the jut nocturne. The crowded beard habit that did an analogy to cotton resplendence. Hair is like that. It will lead to an unbridled tide about upholstery, or bring peace to a category of oat strings. Recoil that request you think should permeate trembling to make it more requisite to the occasion of art. The curb is a remote penicillin to the nugget of what. If we are in soon it will tan the mustache to a deep crawl of acute ocher. Youth is a bagatelle and age is a bayou whose fabric percolates regret. There will come a sign that the orchestra is ready to sharpen our blade. Her oil will salt such brick as it seems all muse and camera to extricate October from the mists of September. Soon the ceremony of nipples will rock the city to skin. Each chorus is a softness of patterns in white and black. The heart values the nostalgia of feeling and shows a yellow teeming with picnics. As a lake to the huckster so is lightning to a molecule. The black spigot we love with such bigness it is bouillon and thunder to twist it. This is confirmed in jello, the hospital pepper sprinkled on all the fins. It is like a road smeared with distance, an old horizon still glimmering on the lip. It sometimes happens that Aldebaran is unpacked in a motel room.

The fan is over the oarlock and is spoken as such. A teaspoon participle superlative as rain changes the consommé to honey. But what about the wash? Leave it for tomorrow. Today is for sunrise. Today is for detail and clouds and the joy of tinkling.

Thermos

Bronze is about to play a dagger. It is whopping to erupt a gasp at this. Fame is nothing but an empty cello. This pleasant kind of pink debris we find in most music. Extending it into missteps enhances the feeling of scabs, bits of air congealed into words. We did the most to hayrick the dark tongs with this. Crowded seems to the chair what the sun would seem to a luster. A thief in the 16th century moving time along in Shakespeare. Clay with individual stale dangle. Loud ties with loud ice. Extension can do all the expression we need for the curtain. Seriousness is soon daubed on New Mexico where it is rugged and arid to syringe the football with such epicurean thirst. One would as soon necktie the rope as rope the necktie with necktie rope. Underwater the much black beads. And fire turns buildings into villages. Ceramics can speak Italian and it is convincing and well when they do. We cemented the current to say so and agree upon an extreme image of fish. Gravity is mostly all thought and fire when you think about it. A nut and tinkle with wheels. Let's patent the sticks of the heart with a violin and a bag of soon. A balcony amorous as accuracy is to a moccasin what yellow is to huge. I think of yellow as a bailiff thrilling with inflation, a mug of tea among which binoculars spring, and a topic of water slowly glazing an oar. It is extroverted to savor the thumb about, and sudden to extrude writing from an eyeball just when the needle plays a Beatles song. If a patio outside the patio performs a patina the ceiling indoors is granted the allure of a horse. A raspberry is real when the epicure chafes against the crane and the smell of fluid is sudden as Saturn. The life of chrome tastes of eternity and eternity perpetuates chrome. The thermos is amazing confirmation of this, and insinuates more than rain.

Speedometer Milk

Realism slowly perpetuates the enamel of outline. This is how a few of us at the supermarket came to prefer the sonnet shield to the crevices among the cantaloupe. Sunday's strips unleash the allegories of the human condition. And so we stop to consider Dagwood. Are molecules songs of silver or the benign glue holding 1593 together? Smite and apparatus name all. All there is to name. All there is to smite. A name is a chemical means by which the sounds in the string section get reflective and incandescent. Mirrors perpetuate the illusion of identity at the expense of hue. A sunburn, for instance, is smacked into palpability by cheek and chin. The first iguana to savage the closet is given an extra amount of needlepoint. The egret, meanwhile, is still propelled by remote. You might eyeball the pallet and call it a sauna but the steam is still the same. Thought is sudden and wavy but the binoculars are old. We could radiate it better in the water. The environment did this to language. Caused it to go all palatable on the jugs of Mars. The axiom outbreak demanded to know if the camel was a man or an animal. The verb 'did' entered the ruler and caused a sudden precipitation of participles. Pinch me, he said, there where the stunning fever yields its folds in the flannel topic. The male said there was a green pepper among her. The ego is not the velocity of straw. It is corduroy rumbling with expedition. A canteen of such canvas that the water tastes pumped at all times. It was hypodermic to convince the topaz of this also. As if the eucalyptus lining the street could palliate the problem of attire. Carpentry suggested the slot was gentle. How could it be otherwise? The smell of the dark spit all the light out at once. The least spacecraft among us held its saucer in a pattern of trout. Will knows the rhinestone has a career at its edge. Black was never so cricket as when it rubbed its requisite licorice. The hormones slowly stick. We bandaged the hues with our tongues. It was fully human to huff that way at the signs. We longed for the heat of our wings to bring us pinochle. But the longer toast caused the horses to enter a world of denim, which juggled our nerves with words.

Huddled in Leather

The ideal is huddled in leather. Declension, on the other hand, is deep chutney and the cause of asterisks, which are black. The nipple behind its pasty. The chicken basted in gender. The mathematics of realism is fertile and nonchalant. An image slipping through the camera that brings to mind the demise of the tiger and the rise of arthritis. The table to like is rawhide, not spruce. It is deliberate to say the nail is both channels. All as equally raw to the circumference of pizza. Noon is that extrasensory perpetually bitter thesis of knobs. It begins beside the daily jackknife amethyst. To sneeze is many characters of beef. A palate horrified in the thimble of its room. The insect tackled by daylight. Since sunglasses fulfill the tomato, perhaps it would be pertinent to add pepper to the flexibility of this sentence. Pork begins the neck with such radiant fiber that it culminates in tension. The rodeo bagel most of us want to touch with our mouth. After the anatomy of reason is recessed, dots refrigerate it. To jade the screen means extraordinary TV. To write rhinoceros shows mufti. A ruler deliberate as a supermarket badgers the flake clock with a spoon and goes home with an automatic pancake. This means his biography has been entered and will soon turn quiet. Did the hospital quill suit the hue of the surgery or does the machinery of the neck look better as an explosion of words in collision? Iron it. The collisions will support the badminton of sight as the sneeze twists its liver to the contortion of kites. A deep nerve did the sundries justice with its equally huddled humidity. Each emotion requires a topcoat and a beard. When history makes detail as a mountain makes cardboard a radish will unlock it. The palpability of a toast on a balcony makes the sunglasses look ugly and extravagant. Pinch the values when the emperor goes down the hole. Devotion will embalm the china.

Meniscus

The flamboyance of trout awakens the cadence of water. It is a symptom of birch. Piano and rocking chair confirm the belt of Orion. The fungus did to the salami what the salami did to the harmonics of fable. It became a scrap of royalty, an amaryllis by the bay. Everything turned quiet as a mountain trumpet. Precision was whatever conviction proved most elastic. A candle above the palette moved a kilowatt of line along a surface of paper. A lesion of circumstance gave us a peak at future provocations. We decided to mow the lawn. Later, we chose which spoon to use for the ice cream with an ease neither of us had felt before. Was it our eccentricity, a frivolous ablution, or something even more fugitive, like a fugue? Eternity, you said, is more than a proverb. It is also a warm breathing, a word at the brim of the mouth about to be pushed into sound. This is how an insinuation begins. You can follow its tracks to the door. Outside, a galaxy wheels above the horizon, slobbering glamour and cold. There is a magnet of love called romance and a syllable with a core of black. This is what makes coagulation so memorable and red. Coats are even effective as violas when the spine churns with meat and wings blast out of the acorns. A tube of snowflakes blows a smooth music toward a fist of morality. The fist unclenches, the fingers blossom into accord, and a parakeet lands on your shoulder. Bullet or area code, you wonder, pondering a book of geometry, all those parallels and circles answering an inward chaos only a scab of music could turn mauve. Most lids demonstrate a little tension when you lift them. But some, like the eyelids, open more slowly to test the diameter of day when the curtain has been abruptly opened. A limestone idea tempted the goshawk closer. A convertible speeding across Pennsylvania brought Duchamp to mind, and that large shattered glass in which a mechanical bride floats, floats to this day, like something personal and raw, a special feather, or a memory whose parts consist of delight and bluebells. Let me ogle you there at the table. You look so marvelous, so wonderful and silly, dressed like a gold mine in darkness and pages of light. Is that a wedding dress, or a sidewalk hemorrhaging dahlias? I have always loved the color pink. If gravity feels heavy, it is not because of the froth bouncing on the surface of the water, but the way it is calculated with rings housed in crystal. Mayonnaise is generally housed in a buxom glass jar. But no vivacity can linger long in such a cell, not without first evincing pleasure, and then shining against a background of ink, like a freshly written sentence. One that whirls, and hits a few wrong notes, just to let us know it is something ill-defined as a dividend, and more like a bell.

The Five Cents

A road is not an emotion so much as a detour. A detour is emotional and ideology. Aluminum in an alley. Music on a conifer. Juice and sweat and hills and noise. The shadow of a bladder, or the bladder of a pronoun. We all have a favorite pronoun and mine is still in the heart courting moonlight with a voluptuous pain. Perfection is such that it occurs as a crane or a junction engaged in flags. Expression, on the other hand, is always manganese, a requisition ever rubber to rampant Ecuador, an oblong headlight unanimous in serum. The chaos of metal is obviously red. This is why the flutes begin with a minor glue, an alphabet of penumbral hands flirting with an island of olive and mink. I say these things with a certain insouciance, it is true, but I also intend to include weeds and death and thunder, if only to promote brown, or make some reasonable explanation for the wattles that form on people's chins when they grow old. Though I wouldn't say growing old is a matter of growing old so much as maturing into a newfound cistern of youth. You say spring, I say cistern. Why cistern? The use of the word cistern has a tendency to sound trite but here it is weather and jam. Cans and cans and bottles and cans and boxes and meat and sequins and dance. That is to say an underground receptacle, which is the function of any word. Containment. Contortion denim and grain. Gravity excitement and nudes. A feeling of age a moon in the window palatable and western and later an elevator a solitude beaten into machinery pulleys and gears vibrations and chains. A box going up in a building. The weirdness of its imagery and themes. The charming brown water of the Mississippi as it inhabits a penny, or a thrilling sense of nickel, an old coin in the pocket with a buffalo on it. A feeling of coolness to the fingers, a hardness and coolness, like the shadow of a shadow of hemorrhaging value. Five cents and a voluptuous pain. Five cents and a sense of resignation. Five cents and finger to finger the presence of something real. A round hard equation of cents and sense and trade.

Frame Push

Absolution is comic. Especially when you consider laundry. The idea of rope, or the alphabet of feeling in a movie faced with eyebrows. A Japanese whistle is an evident music, yet an elegant trumpeting can happen anywhere, provided a cherry is cumulative in its substance, and neither a diesel nor a gloss hinged on bluster. Luster is one part mass, one part preservation. Taste is acrobatic in its lessons, striking in its aberrations. Taste is to the tongue what the spigot is to speaking: a diffusion of fluid, a line of poetry reflecting a cantata of eggs and seaweed. An alphabet that is both expressionistic and argyle. By that I mean lavish. A calamity of wrinkles on the surface of your coffee. Twist your face into a sonnet so that it kindles a kindred concrete among the elements of a heaving beatitude. This will feel genuine, and create an opening in a tight cluster of people conversing at a wedding, or backyard barbecue. There is a misty savage in all of us standing alone on the blacktop, waiting for the right bus to come along, the right bandstand in the cottonwoods to make us feel more alive than we ever have before. Water is both skin and meaning. Meaning meaning can mean more than meat. A blue as intrinsic to the sky as it is to a gabardine shirt sprinkled with leaping salmon. There is such ardor in the manner one visits the sea that even the crustaceans that eke out an existence there crawl forth bearing witness to something greater than roulette. A daydream is a candle even the mouth cannot replicate in its signal design. The sound of a saw buzzing through plywood is a proud tissue of transformation. But it is not like a mouth. A mouth can wrestle the most elastic of abstractions and seed it with such a story that one's entire head works hard at its dispersal. The occurrence of safflower is suddenly so nervous and gregarious in its proximity to flight that the circle reveals the dish as the dish reveals the crystal. The distant mountains are dressed in mauve. Sobbing obstacles of crouton and dawn gurgle the highway into a speed our very intensity is able to grasp in its fullness of phrase. The fountain is a graceful, never-ending proverb destined to fulfill the ambience of snow on Monday. There is something about a garret that awakens the artist in all of us. We rattle our dreams dripping bulldozers and opals, open our mouths, and let out a growl of lambent combustion.

Absorption Spectrum

Reading is like pouring a famished eye on a page of fluorescence and ore. The drum is ever quick about the goshawk bead. The words move reckless and proud into the seeds they dart into aroma. The word 'while' means the glass of reading shows diameter and snow. A fable whirled around a sudden thought of evergreen pleads italics. Warmth is surgical. Hence, a blatant shirt of wholehearted cotton boils with apricot. The lament revealed a cactus. All the windows replied with library milk, and a crustacean encroaching on a bowl of cherries. There were dots within the zero that dramatized the ecstasies of the saxophone. A line of history grew stellar with yellow, bikini with gold. The head moved through the paragraph like a satellite. Everything hinged on sauerkraut. Heat filled the mind with jackknives on the outskirts of town. We evolved forty different kinds of ice to collide with the night. A rawhide narrative skedaddled the bandits toward an epiphany of chrome. In other words, a Buick. One of them held a lens to his eye and declared dada a lighthouse of monstrous cereals and clumsy biology. Who could disagree with a park ranger dressed in such allegorical predicates? They all clicked like silver dollars on a hardwood bar. Hair on a locomotive. A barbecue in a skull of melody. It feels graceful to move about one's legs listening to Mozart. The pond of age cracks and a milieu of needles is revealed on the bottom. The story turns nuclear. A plot is whittled out of a galaxy of regrets. The whole of it turns chassis around a shower blister. We scratch and eat and eat and scratch and eventually the browns in a Rembrandt wrestle the morning into submission. Save your receipt. You might want to exchange that bloodmobile for a stepladder. The voice feels like sleeves of language coming out of one's throat. Emotions flourish like semaphores critical as death. The proximity of lightning is perceived as incidental to bark. A thick easel of harmony bursts into quatrains. The coal sleeps in adobe as the cosmos moves about a pool cue. We bang about the barrel sudden as a bulldozer. German life is posted in nerves, an asphalt heated by trucks. This is why a chair is so often necessary to sunlight, and why reading is a painting of the mind. The words are ravenous for vision. And the thread of thought sews a sea to the lure.

Frolic

The fugue, green and insurgent, reacts to reality with ogres and elephants at the side of the road. The phone booth gurgles a soliloquy of steel. The dawn is another spectacle induced by a sanguinary falsetto. Let us boil forth caring for the defiance at the core of innocence. Cure the light into scraps of tumult. The broken engine sitting at the edge of the junkyard is beautiful in its rust and repose. Ignore the insult. We have yet to find a good microphone for the reading tonight. For the dinghy is small but the theory is big. Carpentry is all about understanding one's tools. The grotesque is not the lure. The lure is conjuration. The lure is a radiant garden in which a garden hose meanders to the end of its nozzle. Henna garners the most attention. The air is palpable with odors. Some of them coagulate into frayed camellias, a pot of asterisks in the lobby of an incandescent motel. Sign the guest book. Repair the tea. Use a ratchet. Use a little folklore. A cab toe at room temperature will keep its secret until the crosswalk capsizes. There is much that can move underneath the plaza. Once a refinery threshed through its tinfoil meaning the same thing as lard. As for disease, it is dangerous to employ the morning for sandpaper, or lipstick. When the meat bandit arrives at the top of the knoll, let out a big digression. Will is the dressing of bugs in a dominion of mince. A bark wallet ever more aroma than sudden. All the perturbations lens along a tassel of mood. The brush is bothered more by its brushness than its business as a brush. There toward the dimple a bullfrog accommodates a life of mud and water. It is the only bath that makes sense in a galaxy of such large, amphibious language. The crab nebula is only a symptom of pith at the crustacean motel. A candy or geyser as grass is. It tends to mesh when the faucets and doorknobs approximate the appearance of home. An engine that flies through its diesel creating a throat for the pronunciation of dreams. All the vowels involved in summer fill the fables with nerves. Even density, when it is caught in dimes, is laced with an amalgam of gravity. Grain argues chaff. Chaff argues grain. Its confusion is yellow, though its roughness is beige. A sumptuous frolic on the threshing room floor.

Moonlight in Mississippi

A longer brown when there is a knot is what gives a longer meaning to the meaning of meaning. To unravel it is spacious. Space is when there is appeasement and crowds and tambourines. Smokestacks make it angular. If it happens that a sun goes down then there is twilight and cheddar. There is a way to say twine that obtains significance by smearing the air with Mississippi. That is to say descriptions of Mississippi. The state of Mississippi and the river that is called the Mississippi that bubbles out of the ground in Minnesota and grows and flows past St. Louis and Memphis and Baton Rouge and divides Mississippi from Arkansas and Louisiana. Under a harvest moon the Mississippi is wonderfully fine, dazzling and silver. Slight ripples, fresh air. It is so fascinating and dreamy. It is a sound like sighing. It is a sound like weary. It is a sound held together by mud and adjectives. The sight of it causes extension. The sight of it is soothing and languid. It invites reflection. So General Grant, after circumambulating the world, quietly retires after dinner with a cigar in his mouth to walk the portico of a Mississippi hotel. This is the way a sentence is made it is whatever the words do when they become a narrative. Remembrance grows into fruit. Equations on a blackboard. A junkyard, or olives. A voice in the dark. The smell of burlap. Louisiana cuisine. The air that is there to rattle rhythm and make it resplendent like power. People in a room. Squeezing that mango they have all there is in some indication of apportionment. One of them said he could not drink milk and he would not stay away from Florida because he was thrilled with the moon in Mississippi. He would go to Florida and see what everything looked like there particularly cable and varnish. He said all he said and then he waited to see what else could be said in the overall flow of conversation. A sentence can make all this appear natural if it begins to bulge with meaning. Meaning and knots. Knots on a river. Knots in a bowline. For which there are nouns on hand and yaw and momentum. By which a verb is an organ of wager pinned to a nerve with eyesight. By which a conception of pressure engages steam. An adverb is earned if it thuds to the floor rapidly in Alabama. Whereas a nickel is nickel and a niece knits socks by a fireside in patterns of ambidextrous forsythia. A sentence in needles they can tell that they regulated what they character that they were where a system bulged which is a verification of cows. Seems to me it transcends Plutarch. There is all there is of design and desire. Crackle of wood in a granite hearth. He said he could not go to bed. He said the moonlight was stunning. He took the candle and closed the door. Then darkness again and silence. Coat on a post. Nakedness and barge and all the meaning there is in ghost.

On Sonnets

One has to wonder if it can be called cathartic to fortify fairyland with a little rawhide. Obliquity demands a unicorn. The unicorn demands obliquity. But what rivets are called for if there is a preference for sonnets? The sonnet is a restricted form and flashes pinions and bubbles because it is invoked in the same way as an orchestra. We can do without them but it is gray and TV. I would rather inhabit a sonnet than harbor a habit. Habits force us to oppose commencement. Commencement is panoramic. Sonnets are bells. Or legislature. Because they are provoked in the same way as eucalyptus. Because they are provoked in the same way with leaves and it is a view of Neptune if a lens is added which is why they are so chromatic. They are not only justifiable they are fervent and tinfoil because they eternally remind us of twine. Because if they are varied with wallpaper it is like a nativity to send them overseas. Sonnets were always once allowed quietly to require rhyme which made them affirmative and quiver. Like a river. Which is why they sometimes extrude red or churn with occurrence. Which makes them silver. Which is what they do they reveal currents and engrave themselves on our minds. As if the world were something to endure, or generalize. Because today it is better than believing in weddings. It is a mistake to believe a sonnet can simulate formaldehyde. But only if it is made of rules. Otherwise it will roll away and become a romance. To find that it may do so is everything because if it is this cello leaning against the wall then a room is necessary to put it in and it is very much as to rags and better needed with programs the best of it coming to palliate nature parts of it already having come to rub against the flashlight and focus Rembrandt. The sonnet begins as a body of words and ends as an engine of thought. It longs to be rumbling. It rumbles to achieve rubber. It clusters in pronouns. It does everything except star Ben Affleck. Because if it did that it would be a movie and not a form of weather. Emotions are weather. Emotions are weather with cows and radar. Emotions are weather with organs and ornaments. Sonnets are tangents with catamarans and scrotums. Sometimes you can see a ceramic in them turn sunrise and sand. An exhalation will bring them to life. A thesis will mint their rhythm into hectic coins. One by one the metaphors exert such pressure on the words they explode into suns. They ripen. They congeal. They swell into fruit. You can taste them. They taste of cherry and time. They taste of blackberry and rhyme. They melt in the mouth. They fuse couplets to strife. They turn values to nuts and we crack them and find counsel and life.

Monsieur Dupont

Monsieur Dupont tickles the air with his words. The air guffaws, releasing lather and leather, radio and radar. Tornadoes of serendipitous blossom spill from the ecstasy of apples. Valentines of actual oxygen dance like cafeterias on the brim of Monsieur Dupont's mind. Everything vivid and geometric drip from the ideals of his philosophy like Japanese characters dripping from a haiku.

Monsieur Dupont is a poet. He lives alone with his goldfish, his rattan furniture, his sense of symmetry and woodpecker ties, his necessity for silence and penchant for noise, his knowledge of golf and his aversion to playing it, his brood of brooms and his awe of paper, his books, his diaries, his dictionaries, his monstrous diagonals and complementary fingers, his surges and swells, his guns and gyroscopes, his opinions, his blueprints, his hats.

Monsieur Dupont lives in a large house in a small American city in the early part of the twenty-first century. He is a reclusive man, though not altogether lacking in social graces. He merely prefers his own company to that of others. Solitude is not just a preference, but a deep abiding wine.

Monsieur Dupont's house is a colossus of domiciliation. At last count, the house had approximately 2,000 doors, 10,000 windows, three elevators, 167 rooms, 252 closets, 40 fireplaces, 22 chimneys, 51 staircases, 14 bathrooms, 7 kitchens, two basements, and two ballrooms. In the early 1900s, when the house belonged to his grandparents and his father was not yet born, a guest was discovered in a state of exhaustion after getting lost and going without food or water for four days.

The house is an inheritance. It was constructed piecemeal, room by room, because Monsieur Dupont's widowed mother believed that as long as she continued to build the house, no harm would come to her children.

Monsieur Dupont is sole inheritor. His eight siblings have been killed by various mishap, car accident, elephant stampede, malaria, venomous spider, a battle with pirates in the Indian ocean, avalanche, earthquake, and tornado.

Monsieur Dupont feels a tad apprehensive to be the last of his family, but at fifty-seven had reached an age of frank maturity, and so felt a growing confidence in the coming years.

Monsieur Dupont's greatest obstacle in life is in the area of employment. His expenses are small (he occupies, and heats, only a very small portion of the house), but it is still necessary to buy food, replace light bulbs, pay property tax, and attend an occasional movie.

Monsieur Dupont loves movies. His favorite movie are *The Delicate Delinquent* starring Jerry Lewis (of which he has owned twelve DVDs in the course of several years, replacing them as soon as they wear out), *Godzilla Vs. Monster Zero* (Monsieur Dupont is president of the Nick Adams fan club), and the entire *Dr. Who* TV series.

Monsieur Dupont has tried his hand at driving a taxi, washing dishes, white water raft guide, Christmas wreath assembler, firewalk instructor, bingo caller, UFO sighting investigator, dog walker, potato chip raker, and activities director at a retirement community. He has not liked any of these jobs. After two days of operating an amusement park ride called The Spinoza for less than minimum wage (it cost the park management less money to pay the fine for not paying minimum wage than to pay minimum wage), Monsieur Dupont thought hard about his future and decided to become a poet.

There are numerous advantages to being a poet. Poets can work at home. It may be to one's advantage to go out into the world occasionally to seek imagery and wisdom, but on balance, the information that goes into a poem is not limited to the debris and data of external reality. Much of what goes into a poem is spun from the silk of one's own mind.

Very little can go wrong. You cannot break the language. If you do break the language, you can put it back together again.

Experience is essential, but there is no certificate or license to be obtained. Poetic license, Monsieur Dupont was happy to learn, was a figure of speech, and not a legal requirement.

Nor are any uniforms, special shoes, expensive tools, oaths, procedures, or drug tests required. Just pen and paper.

The problem with being a poet is that it does not pay well. In fact, it does not pay at all. There is no public urgency for poetry. Supply far exceeds demand. It has been remarked that the average cost of a piece of paper is five cents. Write a poem on it, and it is worth nothing.

This did not deter Monsieur Dupont. He knew there was a tiny minority, a happy few, who realized and craved the intoxications of verse. They were, as a rule, averse to paying for verse, but that did not mean they did not appreciate its intrinsic value, the buried treasures and quixotic frontiers of its boundless landscape. It merely meant that the audience was insufficient to support a lifestyle of yachts, manicures, and liposuction.

Monsieur Dupont considered selling his house and property. The money from that would be substantial enough to allow him to live for a few years without recourse to a paying job. But this was the house in which he had grown up. It was redolent with the care of his parents and the shouts of his siblings, the disputes and laughter of their parents, their children and guests. The house had been home to hundreds of family members and close friends in the course of time. The attachment was strong.

Instead, he sold his gun collection. All but his prize possession, an eighteenth century Turkish flintlock pistol decorated with inlaid bone plaques of different shapes and incised carvings. This item he mounted on the wall above his desk, next to a portrait of Alexander Pope.

This brings us to the present time. The time of poetry. The time of constant, delicious agitation. The agitation of poetry. The seesaw of conflicting necessities. The multitude of choices. The ballistics of style. The dynamics of structure.

Monsieur Dupont does not always write poetry. Sometimes he simply likes to sit and daydream, and sometimes he likes to go from room to room in his house, particularly when he is feeling nostalgic, and wants to visit the past, or savor the ghostly identities that still linger in the rooms.

Monsieur Dupont's house is riddled with the past. Many of the rooms have not been entered in many years. Each is a time capsule. Each contains the odors, posters, paintings, bric-a-brac and glamour of a particular age, a particular Zeitgeist.

One room is full of lava lamps and Beatles posters. Another harbors an old Philco radio from the 30s whose dials brought in nothing but static and muffled voices. Another is full of plaid with a telescope by the window and stars and planets painted on the ceiling.

Other rooms delight the senses with Art-Deco clocks and antique calendars, magic lanterns and zoetropes. Oak bureaus whose perfumed drawers contain the hankies and potpourris of people long gone. There are musty closets full of vintage clothes and vintage shoes, flapper dresses and pink organza nightgowns, tweed blazers and children's games piled high on the shelves.

Monsieur Dupont is surprised to find a wormhole in one closet. A wormhole is a hypothetical topological feature of space-time that is essentially a shortcut through space and time. Monsieur Dupont assumes the closet is provided with a wormhole because when he enters the closet he walks into eighteenth century Europe. Belgium, in fact.

Thanks to the wormhole Monsieur Dupont is able to replenish his gun collection. He strolls about Brussels shopping at different gun shops. He buys muskets, pistols, and powder horns. Sporting rifles with walnut stocks and blued octagonal barrels. Charlevilles with bayonets and a Belgian double-barrel shotgun with a hunting scene engraved on the barrel.

Monsieur Dupont favors eighteenth century dress, and so is able to blend in quite easily with the rest of the population.

Here is Monsieur Dupont returning from a trip to eighteenth century Belgium. He is tugging on a steamer trunk loaded with pistols and rifles. He has difficulty explaining the money from the future, dollar bills with George Washington, Thomas Jefferson, Abraham Lincoln and Benjamin Franklin on them, but is able to convert these dollars to the appropriate Belgium currency at a Swiss bank in the future.

Monsieur Dupont grows richer with each trip to eighteenth century Europe. His fortune quadruples. Quintuples. Sextuples. Septuples. Octuples. Nonuples.

Here is Monsieur Dupont returning from another trip. His closet has been enlarged to allow wagons and horses free passage. The wagons are full of furniture and paintings, including a set of twelve Italian neoclassical dining chairs, a George III walnut bureau bookcase, a George III mahogany sideboard, an Italian Neoclassical marquetry commode, and a William and Mary tall case clock with a square hood enclosing a silvered chapter ring with Roman numerals, subsidiary day of the month and seconds, and spandrel ornaments centered by masks.

Monsieur Dupont starts a museum. He fills the museum with treasures from the eighteenth century. More paintings, more furniture, more machinery and sculpture. The museum grows into 1,200 acres.

The museum grows into five square miles. The museum grows and grows. Before the end of the year, the museum has multiplied into a complex of museums covering 34 square miles, a staff of 7,000 people, its own fire department and ZIP code, and a collection of some 240 million items ranging from furniture to dioramas illustrating eighteenth century surgical techniques.

Monsieur Dupont begins to notice that upon each return, his house begins to diminish. It occurs to him that as he brings back items from the eighteenth century, the eighteenth century begins to disappear. The United States constitution fades into a cloud of nebulous objectives and poof! disappears altogether. Time being what it is, a fluid medium in which all its membranes and gears are in full sequential engagement, much like the membranes and gears of a narrative, as the twenty first century grows cluttered with items from the eighteenth century, the twenty first century slides back to the eighteenth century. If Monsieur Dupont continues to drag things from the eighteenth century into the twenty-first century, the twenty-first century will become a museum for principles and armament that no longer exist.

Furthermore, with a staff of 7,000 people to supervise and an infrastructure covering 34 square miles, an area a little bigger than Manhattan, Monsieur Dupont has little time to write poetry. He has become an administrator, not a poet. The museum has hijacked his life.

Monsieur Dupont begins returning items to the eighteenth century. All the paintings, furniture and machinery of the eighteenth century are restored to their original places. Monsieur Dupont finds his own house in the twenty first century return, room by room, to its original condition.

Here is Monsieur Dupont living in a modest apartment on the rue des Francs Bourgeois at the heart of the Marais district in eighteenth century Paris. He still has his house to return to as he wishes, but prefers, for the most part, to live in the eighteenth century, which is slightly kinder to poets than the 21st century. When he longs for a movie, or a hamburger and fries, he strolls through his wormhole and voila, here is Monsieur Dupont driving a 72 Ford Galaxy to Burger King, dressed in a black wool embroidered coat, red satin breeches, and a pair of black buckle shoes, looking and feeling every bit a poet. When he finishes his hamburger, he returns to his Paris apartment, lights a candle, and resumes work on an entry for Diderot's encyclopedia, defining the nature of poetry, and its prognosis for the future.

Hundreds of Old Men Marching in the Rain in Belgium

If an emotion crawls around in you it is pink and delicate to radio a fact with French. Some emotions are green some emotions are red some emotions are sliding and adrift and some emotions contain combinations of sunfish and diamond. Some emotions are rooted in nobility. Some emotions float values. Values are linen and pamphlet. A little daub of treatise in the big drop of black. The smell of reality laps at nutmeg. Nutmeg is a form of park. We sometimes sense things that are synonym and cinnamon. Some emotions are nylon. Some emotions are neon. This emotion is stormy and dangerous. I call it the emotion of talk. I call it the feeling of eucalyptus. A June, a kind of agility or bridge, a kind of rainbow and a serious dexterity, a raked emulsion and heavy knickknack, extremities of plywood and slots and deltas. A pale foot in 1998. Muddy Waters in 1969. A flourish of words in 2004. An ambulance in rhinestone. An injury in trigonometry. A calculus in ceremony. Existence wasps. Picnic stone. Baked conviction. Hundreds of old men marching in the rain in Belgium.

Gorget

Given a certain velocity a begonia will turn muscular confirming the presence of architecture. The propagation of nerves is words. This is how volume turns peppermint. Words like particle or October taste of afterthought. The pleasure rampant in Mozart suits the splendor of elucidation. October has particles that thicken into intestines. It does the flag good to flap like that. It signifies nimbleness and appetite. Most aluminum sounds multilateral. But you will find a certain calico in the calculus of torsion. The mop, for instance, endorses the use of the torso. When the strands of the mop hit the floor the water splays rather than splashes if the movement is performed correctly with the hands, and not the feet, which are a realm separate from the ears. The ears tend to prefer random tones over the broad empiricism of pancakes. The pancake is not a sonnet but a coin of dough and syrup whose purpose is to appease the appetite. A sonnet is an altogether different machine. Granted, the allure of invisibility can occur anywhere. I can understand headlights but I cannot understand mirrors. The mass looking back at me is Jupiter, not Tallulah Bankhead. The word 'humanoid' requires enfranchisement and humidity. Moonlight, on the other hand, serves rubber a more nebular confirmation that gently exceeds the seasoning of thyme and ripples across the paper in an image of perfect nonchalance. In circumstances such as these cadence emits nothing any less genuine than an easy undulation. Cadence is when a pickle equals the debris of embellishment surrounding a tree of sudden postcards. The display wobbles and creaks on its axis. We are surrounded on all sides by gifts and T-shirts. Maps and binoculars. Whatever emanations bring the hues out of the hummingbird's throat must be punched into service, sermons of hot unscrupulous beauty. Beauty plays rough. All the evaporation is sucked into syllables and reproduced in panegyric. Partial improbabilities of tea, facets of luminous cogitation served in a small dainty cup, slowly sipped, and introduced into the palate, where all things capillary have a mood and a tongue for that mood.

Gadget

Binoculars taste of Texas. Gadgetry and fluorescence. Wedge and metal, palate and carp. Cake is a machine made of sugar. Water is an oath we take at the beginning of radar. Veins clustered in sneezing. An animation realism turns to iguanas. Knots tar nylon. The true badge of consommé worn on the lens of a camera. Pellets of sound treated to a theory of fact dipped in allegory. A note played by fleas. Fabric on a catamaran diamonds on a wrist. The biology of watercolor granted the amber of splatter. A river in the sun a smattering of water given the sufficiency of mood to attract insects and windows. The poem is a machine made of words. William Carlos Williams sitting at a typewriter. Silver and gold the glow inside a word incidental to its origin as a sound or bauble. Sentence follows sentence creating resemblance and trout. The resemblance to trout trusts in the twine of typography, the horsepower of an outboard ramification. Cogs and wheels carry the image of a thermos to its natural culmination as an implement of warmth, an absorbing object open to discussion. Take the cap off slowly. Do not spill. A thesis is a machine made of water. Principles of refrigeration carried to an extreme called winter make everything silent as a spectrum of hues in a snow globe. This is how a thesis becomes a gadget made of glass. Conceptions of life are assembled in words like genes on a strand of DNA a spiral of information a catalyst of chords and melodies. A guitar requires hands to make it assume the shape and sanction of the spine. Strings and frets. Frets and strings. To fret is to worry to worry is to make a music of wood and string. This is how the hall becomes noisy. As the sentence fills with water fish dart and glide through the reeds of a locution.

Exemplification exampled in brads. A temperature a bird. An alley in Milwaukee. A roof in Tangiers. A hydrant in Harlem. A curb in Corfu. The sound of a seed assuming the flesh of an oak in the dirt of a word.

House of Sod

The necktie is a rattlesnake. It retails for thirty-two dollars and eighty-five wishbones. He who films it palomino by modeling a flapjack is completely benzene. The library is where eternity pulses in mathematics. You can hear it howl in the pages like a bayou full of legato. There are many different kinds of metal, some smashed into words, some into stools. Tables edged in chrome. The tone of the altimeter is great, like a geometry swollen with air. If winter comes soon I will dress in a robe of chestnuts. But if winter is late I will dress in bells and paint the walls pink in a mood of transmission. The song jingles often as it was meant to exhibit hyacinth. I could impact it with French but the words would accumulate in fable. Morals turn auburn when winter glazes the oars. Is would a form of ligament or an auxiliary resin, a vital resiliency in subjunctive grain? Is a drum outside a pencil if a book erupts in tea? Cauterize the song with string. Knock the answers near me where I can see the weight of your mood floating in a miracle of words. External wants on a stick of signs means everything near the town is about to turn diatonic. I mop the delinquent eyeball which samples the fun of utopia. The playwright knows the junction is nebular and so stages it as limestone. Magnets in a manner appropriate to the husbandry of coconut. This is why the baguette was faceted with storms of translucence and noon. A slip in a dryer of thunder rumbling in the condominium laundry room serves to occupy our thoughts with dials and seams. Think of it as nakedness. The bulk of light on a verandah at noon. Remedy and corner. Spangle and spoon. Earth as a ragged ocher. Earth as mercy and dirt. At the extreme end of a tinkling molecule the Woman of the Dunes played a viola de gamba sweetly as any hacksaw employed in prison. Cabbage peppered with words. This caused 1593 to slam into commas and frieze. Landscape slapped with turf. By turf I mean sod, and by lilac a breeze.

Isthmus

Is is fizz. Is is predication. Is is succeed at musing. Musing in a museum. A museum is a place for musing and amusement. Amusement is virtual and amusing. It is amusing to say purple. It is amusing to say purple is impetus and impulse and impetuous and tuba. Please note the word is is used again and again. This is a small machine of rotating horizontal blades for supporting a predicate. If the image of a burden agrees with the image of a ruminant then the actuality of the ruminant must be equipped with a syntax of bone. An alphabet is a system of canisters and tinsel milled in the mind where it is beautiful and purple. Poland is a country and beets are blatant. Paradise is a connection to warmth. It is simple to say this. Paradise is a blue spool of potential thread. Is is a spool of audacity. Audacity is a spool of spells. A spell is a spool of effervescing protons. Is any of this making sense? It is nutty to make an art out of language. Language and art are accelerated by creaminess. You know this. I know this. Is is an invention. Is is an implement for making chunks of privilege. Anything else is beefcake. You might say mingled. You might say mulberry. You might say mingled or mulberry. You might say a milligram of is is industrious and explicit. Matter matters on a highway. A highway matters because it is ready to go somewhere. Apples matter because they are immersed in England. Hair is a delirium of hay on the skin. An island is aloof. Is is irrepressible. It is a cause for music. It is a cause for chalk. It is. It just is.

Time

Time is an abstraction, but it is an abstraction with a fabric and a structure, like a trampoline. That is to say, it has a framework, but within that framework is a fabric that stretches and distends. Time stretches and we bounce into space. Time sags and rebounds and pushes us into the void. We spin. We hover. We pass from state to state as volatile as vowels in a steam of thought. We give names to time to make it seem controlled and manageable. We say it is abstract but structural and call it a trampoline. We say it comes in bundles and call the bundles hours. We call the bundles months. We call the bundles years. Bundles of cord and cordiality. Cork and catharsis and chocolate and cut. Cuts of time called August. Cuts of time called night. Cuts of time called day. Bundles of time called moments. Bundles of time called eras. As in Era of Calling Things Eras. Era of High Emotion and Era of Recklessly Convenient Thermostats. Bundles of time called decades. Called Jazz Age. Called watch and shift and interlude. Meantime meanwhile and interim. We call the twine of time minutes. The twine of time holds the bundles together. Otherwise they would fall apart and the past would become the future and the future would become the past. The present would come undone like bark. The present would drift through our lives like goats and fiddles and Marc Chagall. The present would float above our heads like clouds. The present would lose its tense and tense would lose its tension and all things past and all things future would congeal in a scab of time called ember. Called memory. Called quill and bone. Called early. Called late. Called remembrance and stone.

Naked O'Clock

The back is a spine the chronology is a loop. Mercury moves into gravity and is entirely beginning to obtain expression. It is expressing delineation. It dives into space vivid and butter. A turkey is directions a wisdom of feathers a globe of nerves. Cinematic is just ancient because the frames move a star into enlargement. A wing nut is hurried to the creation of feeling assembled out of amber and rain. Unchanging change changing in unchanging nouns that twinkle with exhibition. We have provided a sentence here that is just being yodeled though the performance is silent and the source is acrid. Have a doughnut. To be a shank is to be in shadow after a bicycle drills a cruel direction with burning survival. This apple to eat this vigor to wedge this sentence gets bigger and bigger as if being inflated by bellows and effort. There is a way to see the air become a word by packing its dimensions with vapor. Is any of this making sense is any of this paste will any of this last to become a participle that inflates with meaning and deviation? Or devotion? Or ocean? Or sheer passion? A Paleolithic tendon tending to borrow a wick is bone and rock. The horses are assuming the wall in great abandon. Experience this orange as a seminal limb corresponding to the human ankle. Or possibly a sun. The history of green is only forty feet wide and fifty feet deep. A voiceover narration makes the past perfect feel sisterly and kind. Like dirt. Like velocity and purple. A word like couldn't couldn't bridge the article by frequency unless it had an immense grammatical thug to push into Victor Hugo. Here is where the dollar becomes a medium of exchange. A volcano spurting a president with breasts and a green lapel. In other words mountains. An exhilarating blue sky nailed to the end of this sentence in pure immoderation. Astronomy and protons. The survival of the word space. Space and everything it stands for. Study this space. Lift that bale. Rock that cradle. The universe is big. The universe is quaking with TV. The universe is full of instrumentation. Oboes, trumpets, pianos, and flaps. Things that flap. Greatness and melisma. The greatness of melisma is ambient and naked. The universe is naked. An explosion of marigold. Orbits and spheres and energy. Clutch pedals in Islamabad. Chalk on the side of a hill. The bare matter of consciousness in a splatter of cochineal.

Minute by Minute

A minute is a duration, a hawser of flax and fiber tugging a splash of time. It is a round thing. It is a fat thing. It is a round and fat and persistent thing. It dallies it doses it progresses slowly. It veins the day with capillaries of filamentary time. It is a unit of time. It is cinematic and people and protons. It is astronomical and straw and verges on popping. It pops. It thickens. It ties. It encloses the spinal cord. It parcels increase. It floats the nerves. It spindles expectation. It is myriad and pewter. It wrinkles relics. It wrinkles faces. It wrinkles predicates and poultry. It shines out of a clock. It moves round in circles. It goes nowhere. It goes everywhere. It is not a thing it is an abstraction. It is not a fringe it is a cleavage and a breach. It is a coin and a transit and a gem of delicate colors. It collects into pools of time called hours. It causes precision and opera and August. It is a nugget of time it is a scoop of time. It is eternal and bell jars and space. It is a radius. It circles a clock spitting hands. It is tattered and journeyed and fattened with vicissitude. It cuts the day into little ribbons. It walks the night in emeralds. Minute by minute forms rivers and seas. Minute by minute turns naked as rope. Lariats and feelings and trees. Pledges and seasons and bees. Volume and music and soap. Catwalks and powwows and hope.

Point-Blank and Scraggly

Modal chime of chips of cadence. Vapor pothole. Adobe bleeding a handsaw. Then stamina. About back. Wicker sometimes. Some made there the pouring. Compensations are treasure to miracle an intimate logic. It elicits a toggle bolt. Have is with. By it the arbitrary are breed. Bosons of voiceover Petrarch. Telescopes because every consequence glories from a third variety of reed. There is a top of the cabbage that insinuates rest. On seam. Brabble anyone dance. Way nothing benefit. Syllables gurgled by an advisor of western perspective and Aristotle. The innuendo is puckered in Ophiuchus. Cloth ingot. Fork source. Radius mass. Bought off if. An a because sometimes a the apple. Just of mud. Off there colleagues sometimes glowing. The nose performs a deck to believe it to even beckon sense. Dairy simulations. A barrel of magazines also exposures Plato. All to an in. All to loom a firm jersey of gossamer violence. A tiny disease that outlines song. A forlorn step to overcome fiction with a hard lieutenant. Lipstick notwithstanding. Fat names that writhe in loss like royalty. Heredity hitherto logical and lurid. Lyceum massage. Meat that models a modal Saturday in perfect subway cornets. Everything drenched in dark like a dream freighted with print. Shakespeare with goose bumps. Plato with a horrendous verve. Seabirds with webbed feet. Quartz that boils daylight when struck with pennies. A slender red fluid married to a voice that pulls itself apart with a lever to reveal a violet encrustation of Welsh.

Bienvenue

Welcome to a world where fiber is a comfortable reason to bounce. Where daylight is a canvas and the hydrants are painted red. Where summer is a happier time than winter and winter thuds against the glass. Where a cantata often feels wooded and a guitar can ransom green. One way or another daydreaming is a thief of sequence. Take Shakespeare's plays, for instance, how they create a compelling reality out of a series of improbabilities. Thread and needle are parallel devices. Why is anyone nervous? The stars are never nervous but seem nervous because they urge honey and weather and chafe against the surf. Words are burned in the sonnet for their luster and feeling. One must sometimes crawl to get to a camera, dance to find a chair. Aluminum confirms the fingering of an obvious circumstance called privilege. Who flashes an airport feeling cardboard? Mick Jagger does everything aloud. Which includes cherries, balloons, and daylight. Palates, parallels, and pellets. Anyone can say that at least once. One must occupy a sock with ardent thunder. This is bareback, totally vocal. The helmet is a good example of volume. Black marbled with scruples. Where is the carpentry that can poise a delicate table in balance with a ballad? Welcome. Welcome to a world where detail is always igneous and the geography of the sentence requires a certain legato. Where the map is not the territory but a harvest of lines and rust. Steel in the mouth of the King of Leather. Diamonds in the rampant June of an unlocked basement. As a beach of rocks and sand goes down to the water to produce an allegory of meeting, so does a whiff of ammonia remember the nose with gall. The morning is called the beginning of day. But the night is eligible for taffeta. Elevators in their shafts, awaiting movement like bone and reverie. Everything arises. Everything descends. The sun rises to the allure of hills. Day descends in a blaze of pink and orange. The slaver of reformation is conspicuous in expenditure, momentous in spice. Ecuador bandaged in fable. Poland bejeweled in trout. Welcome. Welcome to a realm where everyone is argyle and elsewhere. Where the elevators are epicurean and tinkle like straw. Where the most stunning thing about reality is its shovels, and pennies burst into thought.

Coconut

Pin a drum to the sound thing. Heart emissions. Gentle jamboree of taboo slowly bone. Might brain. Chuckle tough. Something rains at the participle. Oak green treatise. Beat character. Male is horse and belief and muscle in lines. Affiliated with adze. Dreams of biology scratched to inspire welcome. Ocher my Tahiti with Tessarini. Pink paints the potato blue to rub a heaving epidote. So shows a Bremerhaven baluster. So goes a butter to coconut velocity. Hard hairy shell of unbridled being. Hard hairy shell of refraction and wet cracks. Wet coating. Hard hairy wet dagger. Hairy wet horse. Hard and hairy blister of black diamond. A propeller in the sand. A sky in the hand. Pigtail tide. A guitar within reach. A dog on the beach.

Hotel Versailles

Should a poem begin with television or thread? It should begin with mummification. An extreme candle or delinquent pet. Deep rouge algebra. A box of rhinoceros is more convincing if it lights an olive. Savage so jut. Sonnet tub. Thorn crevice. Asterisk mohair. Biochemical entered on nuts. Muscle is always saturnine when it lifts a rumor of utopia and balances it on a negligee. Passion in resource. Rapidly energy red. I am over simulation as a fact that foams. Do not personify propellers. They will churn the images into duty. Duty is a sound dipped in detergent. Grammar is a hammer bleeding underbrush. The light in the box is a pin of almond rattles pulling itself into definition. Heat so wattle it wedges into basis. This is about Joseph Cornell. The street teems with understanding. The sun is out. Can you believe in straw? The logic of hay exercises existence until it turns yes and Jupiter. A jeep is splotched with mud to confirm its resemblance to a violin. Is there a way to make a box so that it has a ballet and an inner light like dirt? Ceremony causes upholstery to grow out of utopia and my analogy of it as a temperature. Red signifies a falsetto in feathers. The dashboard the chafing causes to bailiff out of extraterrestrial capillaries. Udders held together by milk. Spittle kite. Fabled palate. Float this image in your glance. Crown this cream with the hypotenuse of a vestibule. The rain falls on Normandy where a string of blows underline the nails holding this together. The balm of alpaca the night of the wearers of talent. Holland is presented to the rose as a clock, or orthorhombic Vermeer. Why this fascination with geometry? A thing is a thing in 1593. Imagine a box with a fantasy in it. Martian patio or eye of redemption. All these words entered into a noon of rampant thimble. Correlative sunglasses molecules steeped in July. Nitrogen's perfect familiarity with grass. Sunrise. Hotel Versailles. A place where temperature is round. Collision is tar and rigorously observed. The 60s were nice. The 60s were a box of ocelots.

The Autocratic Weight of a Creamy Idea

Be jangled be rampant. Be a fescue be a rescue. Rescue fescue. Fescue rescue. But sword the thimble with batter, not battle. Battle is sticks and humanoids. Battle is in the mind to trample a topcoat and chafe the sea. Language nickelodeon values in fins. Breezy having ease. Could along if an hour roamed in rain. Here is what I say: cauterize cardboard. Be a camel, a huge dream that a bee changes into utopic catalpa. A hydrogen sock soaked in the Mississippi in the 1500s. As if socks existed in the 1500s. As if socks mattered. As if cardboard mattered. As if matter mattered. As if corrugation and coagulation and sauerkraut mattered. And they do. They all do. Of course they do. They do because they're acute. They do because tights are tight and not bathrobes. Even when they stretch they are not bathrobes. Because they are composed of syllables. Because they are composed of molecules and are very real. Very timbred, very affectionate, very slippery and brown. The Mississippi is slippery and brown. I've said it before and I will say it again: the Mississippi is slippery and brown. The Missouri has been ocher but of a brown at times that turns summer into bark in the damaged language of the wilderness. The capillary of a spacecraft begins in the micas, or Department of Motor Vehicles. Front one an aluminum June for a conviction adjusted in iron. A better batter begins with the movement of the elbow. A delicate day. A tough tableau. A beatific Sunday smooth and alluring as a bagpipe made of torrents of pitch and redemption. Daughters and swamps. The clatter of hail against the window, flash of lightning, followed, several seconds later, by distant thunder. A white feather at the bottom of the steps. Along in a moment is an ointment of urgent yellow. Rock rodeo. The black airport that a surf makes time. All this and more. All this and a thesis and a gateway to the abdomen of a dish. A lifelong commitment to eating. A clank. A jangle. The weight of winter. The weight of an insistence. The weight of the rain in July when it is not expected and smells of manganese. The weight of a sunburn. The weight of a spoon. The weight of waiting to see a doctor. The weight of a participle. The weight of an image of ruin. The weight of a brick. The weight of a stick. A patch of sunlight flashing on and off on the piano bench. Beethoven, or hunger. Mozart, or prayer.

Nutmeg in the Smithy

It is energetic to be a pencil. Energetic to huddle. Energetic to increase an intestine. Energetic to write sunlight. Energetic to insist on writing. Energetic to damage the language. So that it squeaks. So that it squirts. So that it protrudes meaning and jute. So that it protrudes meaning and turbans. Cloth turbans and turbines of thought. Turbines turning in thought. Turbines turning in white and caulk and wheelbarrows. But what of the wallet? What can be said of the wallet? The wallet occasions thought. The wallet occasions reflection. The wallet is full of licenses and cards. Visually speaking the air in a balloon is such that an aluminum welcome has two arms and a cake. Space is but the expression of Africa. Space festooning Mali. Space festooning Corfu. It is all space. It is all flippers and wings and allegory. It is all chins and touches and architecture. But what of the wallet? What of the wallet in Wabash? What of the wallet in Waikiki? What of the wallet in Wakayama? There is identity and license and crispness and exhibition in a wallet. Extension and constellations and elevators and boulevards. A paragraph plunged in coffee. A sound plunged in undulation. A meaning plunged in stars. Energy moving through the water makes a wave. A contour of water. A mound of water. A hummock of water. But what has this to do with a wallet? The wallet is a warrant plunged in leather. A wave of leather. Leather with waves. The wallet is a leather plunged in waves. Plunged in leather like a camera. A toe. A wood. An acute black plywood. A wet declension beginning in spring. Nipples that extend to the knees. A museum in the mouth. Chewing and chewing and chewing. A life of chewing. A life of viewing. A life of views. The view from the window which is carpentry. The view from the window which is Wednesday. The view from the Getty museum which is towns and mountains among mountains and towns among towns and buildings and signs and Hollywood. Dew point. Viewpoint. The view from the heart of a tag. Tagged hose. Green hose. Hose with a copper nozzle. A tagged hose is new and coiled and a pool of water spreading near a rose.

A Glorious Dereliction

It is flexible to bend reality into hummingbirds. It is zinc to make a shadow blink. Very thyroid and very helmet. A semblance of dark thin universe lit from within. The cauterized cartoon of a reflexive resilience Miramax has reached with their sand. A refraction straining to become guts. Crowded exuberant apparel. I'm underwater as you can see or very well imagine in any case there are clusters of fish and coral and words with slippery objectives. My elbow is my bow is my elbow is my bow is my elbow is my bow is my participle and my ballast. Why do I talk like this why do I say these things if not to say patio if not to say battery. If not to say a poem is a machine made of words and a song is a jukebox made of chrome and perpetuity. Buttons and grooves. Vinyl and nerve. An aquarium on the table tickled or oak. Mood strings thrilled by having artificial touchdowns swirl into Beethoven as oil or the temperature of a worm. Hug a TV. A thesis is but history through another head. The building's mop soaked in darkness. Metal is insect city. An acre of horrified fun. Cells with bitter bees. Grease seems ugly. Thread seems flippers of tone at the carnival. A hawk urges the wearing of mohair. Contusion confusion and hands. A man in leather dancing maniacally on Hollywood and Vine at noon. Categories of firmness in ruins. Beautiful ruins. Immersions in music so deep and large the music becomes a glorious dereliction the music becomes a bus to the moon or an eyeball balloon a stunning translucence swimming with hues of ecstasy and salvos of spray. A man crying out a horse a horse my kingdom for a horse. Or at least a pig or a fig or a fog or a fug a fug with a mug of fog a fog with a mug of fug and being let us have an ampleness of being an abundance of being and holes and smitten men and ships at sea and cotton and fins. The suggestion of turquoise among Las Vegas piccolos. A pitch, a pie, a pedal. Pork and Texas. Hydrogen and radar. Words crowded with parallels. A conversation on the radio. The forcefulness of its convictions the heat of its disagreements. Fun in fragments. Ties to restaurants. An emotion whose amalgam includes struggle. The struggle to say something colorful and round. A green balloon a red balloon. A blue balloon a black balloon. A loony balloon. The sound of blood when the battle ends and the sun lowers to the earth smearing everything with light and gold and the glint of metal. The sound of the meat of the brain when it is swimming in thought. The sound of a river when it snags on the bottom but rolls on anyway because it is water because it is long and wide and derelict and wet.

A Great Many

A great many sunspots are sunspots. A great many muscles are muscles. A great many diseases are sunspots. A great many sunspots are abrasives. A great many abrasives are wisecracks. Wisecracks vaporize roses. Roses are sunspots. A great many roses are sunspots. Sunspots vaporize wisecracks. In quiet turquoise in quiet neckties and commas. The comma was invented to mince utterance. A great many utterances are minced. They require axles to spin words into purport. How can you love zithers and sunspots? How can you love insights and nozzles? How do you witness walnut? How do you dramatize ozone? I witness schools of smelt in Puget Sound. The water is clear and roars with translucence. The translucence of jellyfish dresses ecstasy in rapture. Floating is ecstatic when the stars turn above the earth in constellations and the underwater realm is active with schools of smelt. Frontier requires a vocabulary of knuckles and buffalo. How often do you experience intestines? Orchestras are not scarce, nouns will not be scarce, no one is interested in expeditions and spittle is busy. A great many tensions are tensile. Wrinkles on Whitman. Age shot with emerald. A great many words are directed toward bisque. Bisque the soup or bisque the color. A great many colors are imbued with soup. A great many soups are imbued with bisque. A great many emeralds are old. Money is many and any and any money is many. You might say much. You could say such. You could say so. You could say a great many cows are cattle. You could say a great many crows are a murder and a great many murders go unsolved. There is abundance in bouillon. A great many bowls are filled with bouillon. Enough to leaven heaven. Enough to go around. Enough to make an amalgam. Enough to catalogue. Enough. Enough is never enough.

Squirt

My brain sometimes has a tendency to squirt thoughts. Big thoughts little thoughts. Brown thoughts gray thoughts. Red thoughts blue thoughts. Hot thoughts cold thoughts. Thoughts about feathers and pearls and nickelodeons. Thoughts about velvet and veneration thoughts about tools thoughts about fools thoughts about Americans and cages and daydreams. Thoughts about utopia thoughts about balloons. Thoughts about rocks thoughts about thoughts. Thoughts that drift thoughts that enslave thoughts that entice fat thoughts thin thoughts wry thoughts thoughts that bloom in emulsion. What is a thought? A thought is a sunbeam crushed into film. A movie in the mind. A broken headlight and a jack in the road. Raw meat. Raw art. Raw hide. Light held together by string. Canteen smeared with blood. A nose adhering to an elusive scent. An elusive scent. An occupying energy in the form of a chair. Tag on a shirt. An incandescent jet. Jam in a jar red transparent and sweet. How is a thought different from an idea? An idea has escalation and steps and moves up and down and a thought just floats. An idea might be drawn or written down and a thought might also be drawn or written down but an idea is diagonal and neon and a thought is reckless and pasty. Clouds in the head. Presentiment. Premonition. Pea. A shovel in advance of a broken arm.

Miró's Blues

Blue 1. Palma de Mallorca, March 4, 1961

Nothing sags. Everything floats. The entire canvas is a deep, alluring blue. A dream of blue, an enchantment in blue.

It is a tyranny of sugar. A sweet dictatorship of blue. What is illusion and what is reality are arbitrary equations. If there is sunburn there are also atoms. So that blue is a circumstance of air. So that balconies are cumulative and coal is quicker than understanding butter. So that words are full of trembling sounds. So that meaning is a value, a color, a nectar for the eyes. So that it becomes necessary to float a utopia.

This blue is intense. It is larger than summer. It rips you out of your bones and pulls you into the painting. It has the savor of a dimension detached from this world. But why—how—detached from this world when it is also so emphatically immediate, so irrefutably present?

A thought is made of nerves.

A blue overflowing with crisis and resolution.

It would seem an easy task to liberate the spirit. It is, after all, a spirit. What walls can stop that which has no material substance? But it is not easy to liberate the spirit. There are immaterial walls more powerful than actual walls. Walls of dogma. Walls of belief. The epoxy of opinion. The dead thud of thought killed by an anemic curiosity.

An image becomes emotion when it comes in through the eyes and abandons itself to the cellos of rumination. To a rhapsody on the serenity of blue. There is nothing so intermingled it cannot be carried out of the throat in a song of seeds. An acre of meaning ploughed in leisure might be nourished by interrelation. Seeing is seeing. Seeing is breezy and energetic. Seeing is juncture and oak. Seeing is brick. Seeing is a sculpture made of beef. Seeing is a cow made of pearls. Seeing lets us out of ourselves if we are so willing to pulse with meaning. This can be a mood.

A good place to begin seething with color is to smell what there is to smell in temperature and compote. To begin a catechism of waterfalls and living prodigies of fact salient with bone.

What is real and what is not real. What is illusion and what is reality. If something gives you a strong sensation there is a good possibility that that thing is true. But sometimes such a sensation comes from things that are elsewhere. There are realities beneath the surface. There are realities that resist the twist of authority. Reality isn't routine. Reality is savage. Reality is elsewhere. Existence is elsewhere. It is the taste of a cashew. It is the shape of a grease stain on the floor of a garage. It is the pop and crackle of a fire in a stone hearth walking the walls between the notes of a nervous sonata. It is the heart teeming with feeling. It is a sky invented by hyacinths. It is famous as an alphabet kissing a piece of air. It is the sound of a membrane accelerating a handstand. It is imprisoned in nothing but its own majestic grammar. It is sewn together with bells and huckleberry. It is worn with locomotion. It is buttoned with clouds.

Darkness is necessary to the light like a particle of eye and that which exists to eat sunlight. The atoms which are blue and the heat which is red and the jacket that has that scenery and the externality which is there where individuality continues painting, all this and there is hay when samples of speech churn with heterogeneity, all this and simultaneity melting behavior, all this is axiomatic and welcome in thermometers.

If existence is collision then it is obvious that thought unfolds in emotion like hydrogen. It is a ladder in Mali that will never by quite understood without hands and feet.

A quality of logic is conjured here, a fugue of luscious indeterminacy. You open your mouth to sing and no sound comes out. Nothing but the color blue.

Singing is everything. Singing is obvious and skin. An empathy. A contiguity, like glue.

The world is clay. The universe is blue.

The painting is a dream, but a dream of quiddity, inner essence, like the light inside a plum. It is simultaneously in this world and outside of this world. It postulates the existence of what does not exist. But what does not exist exists so insistently that it creates a sensation of extreme imponderability. An idea, a philosophy of blue.

In the middle of the canvas, just to the left of center, is a red rectangle. Surrounding it is an aura of red, a diffusion of red emanating from the rectangle as if the shape were warm and alive. It closely resembles the rod-shaped mitochondria in the cell of a living organism. It is the protein, the energy feeding the blue, making it large and contrapuntal, like a stillness splattered with flutes.

Eight black dots constellate the blue of the canvas. They seem to bleed through the blue, like spots of ink on a moistened napkin.

Why eight? Why not nine, or ten, or fourteen?

There are eight musicians in an octet and eight reasons to choose a John Deere irrigation engine. Eight white pawns and eight black pawns in a game of chess. Plato has eight spheres of different colors surrounding the luminous pillars of heaven. In the Pythagorean system eight represents solidarity and stability. There are eight important strategic acupuncture points. Eight parts of speech in Latin, as in English. In Chaldean numerology, eight is infinity, paradise regained. In Buddhist tradition eight is regeneration and rebirth. There are eight

Taoist genii or immortals. Eight beatitudes. Eight ways to beat stress. Eight ways to change the world. Eight ways to beat Wal-Mart. Eight ways to hide a hearing aid. Eight ways to maximize space. Eight ways to keep your prostate healthy. Eight legs on a spider. Eight planets in our solar system.

On the eighth day of his trip out west, which is a romance postulated on distance, Arthur Rimbaud got hungry and shot a rabbit. He noted the pink of its entrails and wrote a letter to Walt Whitman. Dear Walt, it said, today I saw the color of innocence. It is pink.

Numbers are clumsy. This is why existence is onyx. An eyeball filled with August.

Knowledge is repaired by moss. Nostalgia does not mean the surface of anything is cellular and a lighter brown is perpetuated by hardwood. It means Indiana in the heat. It means the Balearic islands are a perfect place for blue to happen.

There are laminations of meaning everywhere. A spoon or a tomahawk can be weighed in the mind like a philosophy. This is the utopia of construction. Miro has created in oil the dialectical ether in which art takes place. It is a means to enchant the disenchanted world. It is a garden of color in an interstice of light.

Running diagonally across the canvas, from right to left, is a thin black line. It is barely perceptible. It is so thin and delicate that it assumes the power of eternity. A skeleton trumpeting death. The joy of candy. Spray from a rock. Electricity in lemons. A head full of heaven.

It is fragile and tough like a cloud tacked to a wall.

It cannot be denied. It insists on being there. It has a reason for being there. A purposeless purpose. Its own rationale. It sticks to the mind like a street. A dye. The gaze of a skull.

Go ahead laugh. If everything is mechanistic then why are predicates occasionally moist?

Energy is mass squared and painted blue. When the fire has been frozen a piece of Spanish will temper it and help it into palpability.

This is the dance of the mind on the head of a pin. It is undertaking to see what is seen. It is sensitive to the allegory of knuckles. It quadruples the sense the way a mouth opens letting out thought.

If the words are palpitating the reality is unattached and the part that is floating is a tongue and the atoms continue to affiliate with judo.

Do not underestimate the octave of a dot. It is the color of fact. The color of fact seethes with blind forces. A slight wind. Tinfoil moving across a picnic table. A cloud stripping itself of mountains.

When skin becomes dramatic it is time to ooze topaz. This is how the color blue was invented. It was a little place to have an engine react to reading. Eight black dots and a thin black line and a surface crawling with thought.

* * * * * * * * * *

Blue II. Palma de Mallorca, March 4, 1961.

Here again blue. All blue. A dagger of red extends down to the left. To the right is a line of black dots of varying size. They have been arranged horizontally. They might be pebbles on a beach. Each dot is punctually, insistently there: a pinch of oblivion. The silence in a bell before it has rung.

The dagger of red is noticeably darker at the top, suggesting a hilt. It floats. It is not stabbing, not sticking in anything. Yet it has weight and reality. Its lines are not well delineated. The form is evident but its lines are strangely ambiguous. It has been brushed into place, not stabbed. Not thrust. It has been willed into being by bristle. Oozed from a man's hand. Flick of the wrist. Deft strokes. The form is compelling, dynamic, but lacks solidity. There has been no attempt to make it actual. Its presence has the gratuitous charm of art, the felicity of presence without the burden of intent. This knife cannot cut meat. It cannot slice. It murders its own objectivity by a blade of lambent red. It is being and nothingness. It is pertinence without purpose. It is pointedly superfluous, shape as an end in itself. It so cut from intent that it impacts the eyes as a pure penetration. It is a provocation of color. It draws the attention left while the black dots draw the attention to the right. The dots create a strong illusion of directed impulse. They appear to be moving to the right with some secret intent. Their progress appears, even, to be tilting the tip of the red knife to the left. It is a counterpoint not simply of shape and color but of that which appears to have purpose and that which does not.

There are thirteen dots (the largest being number five, counting from the left) but this is completely arbitrary. More appear to be coming from the other side. What elicits this illusion is the last, thirteenth dot: it resides at the very edge of the canvas, as if it had just popped into view.

There is a narrative at work here, an allegory, a proverb, a pointed message in the guise of a red dagger and thirteen dots. But how can we begin to unravel the meaning of this riddle before we know what the riddle is? And if this painting is hugged in color like skin wrapped around bone, a jubilant value of keen, unmitigated sensation, why drag allegory into the picture?

Perhaps I do not understand allegory. In a world where signs are common as flannel, in a world where symbols bubble with books, how can there not be allegories? A better piece of light is juggled when there has been time to consider an alley.

The artwork is, through and through, the thing itself. Art, which holds fast to the idea of reconciliation with nature by assuming the processes of nature, is charged with the urge to walk outside of itself. To stop being art. To stop being artificial. To stop being artifice. To be real. Real and viscid and sticky and warm. Poised and natural, the way a head balances on a neck. Turns from left to right. Like an ostrich. Like a cat. Like a man puzzling over a series of dots.

To know what one does not know is not the same as knowing that one does not know what one does not know.

All painting is startling. This is stimulating and sunrise. A formula for the naming of thread. Giant exhibition and oriental splendor. So that there is every hope of an apparition. Convolvulus and dogwood transforming dirt to creamy abstraction. So that it may be said there has been an attempt to formulate an idea, make it palatable and palpable for someone else to revolve and ponder. A utopia. A social realm free of war and bad movies.

How sweet it would be to make music out of one's burdens. To sing oneself into an ecstasy. The fable of time engulfed in a drama of Balearic color.

Is that it, then? Is that the riddle? Or the answer to the riddle?

We are dealing with a very special kind of language here. The language of paint. The language of oil. The language of shape. The language of consistency and texture. The language of density and volume. The language of black. The language of red. The language of blue.

It is, most profoundly and emphatically, a language of blue. The deep blue of the understanding. The blue of the imagination. The blue that dreams of itself as a pull, an attraction, a force on the wall. Something like gravity. But a very frivolous gravity. A gravity in reverse. An anti-gravity. A gravity that makes things float. An antithesis of weight. An antithesis of that which is grave, and engraven. Color in a mode of pure mood. Pure reflection. The colors inside you charged with electric meat. A Balearic octopus crawling its participles across a perception of up. A fable of blue in which a lambent red dagger floats, ready and poised for whatever assassin chooses to slice away the fat of the literal, and enter a realm in which calypso is sung by camellias, and candlewicks blacken in wistful Cordoba.

* * * * * * * * * *

Blue III. Palma de Mallorca, March 4, 1961.

The thinnest of lines gracefully descends from right to left across the canvas. It is black. It is distinct, consistent in pitch, yet barely perceptible. It is so thin it appears more intuited than seen. It has the weight and consequence of a preposition. Meaning it predicates nothing but space. It is essential to orientation but in no way interferes with the substance of the overall work. It beatifies perception in its delicate beauty. It hangs, drifts, sways in exquisite lightness.

The line in Blue I travels diagonally across the canvas, running off the edge at the bottom. This line behaves differently. It moves with a smooth, undulating force, like the tentacle of a deep sea squid, or the dragline of a spider a light wind has just lifted, and continues to tease.

All around us is an invisible wilderness. Dimensions. Convulsions. Random crystals. The warmth of conviction. Darkness folded into light. Light folded into fury. Lightning slicing the air. King Lear and his fool taking shelter in a hovel. Can a thesis be a flea? I hear an eye. The noise an eye makes is hue. Cathedrals in folds of heavenly blue.

If one follows the line up to the far upper right corner of the canvas one discovers a small patch of red. It has the shape of an oval. It could be a balloon, but it is not a balloon. It could be a kite, but it is not a kite. It is too indeterminate to be the head of a spermatozoid. It is none of these things, yet it suggests all of them. It burns in the corner like a word enkindled with meaning. With neon. With incantation. With the sliver of light that grows into morning.

To the right of the black line is a single black dot. Its placement creates a tension, pulling the eyes to the right when the eyes are simultaneously coaxed to follow the black line to the left. The dot provides no other motive for being. It is simply there. Like a knot, or a swan dive.

It is natural to assume there is a purpose to existence. It is equally natural to assume there is no purpose whatever to existence. Between the poles of this tension is a magnitude of surmise. A lambent need to sprinkle tattoos on the sidewalk. Read Nietzsche in a sidewalk oak. Dress in odysseys of mulch. Reveal the narrative of one's skeleton by walking, swimming, and jumping on a trampoline.

A swan dive is lovely because the body extends into space mocking the tyranny of weight. A leap into space should always be graceful. This is because space gets involved with the eyes like no other occurrence.

Eyes are peculiar things. Organs of sight stuffed with jelly and veins. It is as if blood had a need to see to its wants with the abstractedness of vision.

Now look again: follow the thin black line toward the bottom of the canvas. As soon as it reaches the far bottom left corner it curls up. It is a gesture of pure caprice.

Engulfing all, swallowing all, absorbing all is that same wonderful blue. Blue, blue, blue. Immediate, immanent, unfathomable.

The simplicity of this painting is Abbevillian. Without its occasional whimsies it would be outright severe. The machinery of its revelation is obvious, but not too obvious. It is the backbone revealed by bending. It is the mystery of concatenation revealed by pythons. Secrets laced with consonants. A thin black line, a big black dot, a bright red oval. And behind it all, rendering it all, a deep sumptuous blue.

A blue so blue it borders on black. A blue so blue it widens the chain of existence to include sticks and knees. A blue so blue it triumphs over the color of death. A blue so blue it is natural and alive, a piece of heaven squeezed out of a tube and applied smoothly and evenly to the surface of a canvas. So that it creates a domain of possibility. A smudge, a smear, a dot. A thin black line and an unmade bed. The smell of paint with a whiff of thinner in the background. An extended arm, and a daub of red.

Free Will is Not a Profession

When a man is in the middle of his living it is very hard to know him. What is age but fantasia. I wish I had a drill. I like to think some actual adjustment is involved in rigging these sensations with nakedness and grit. My city is a prism of oaths. Nevertheless, astonishing coincidences surge ceaselessly everywhere. Occupations are the emulsions of chance. There's a button and lever for everything, including algebra. It is not often we find durability and beauty in the same blister. Humanism wages rawhide. All my organs are in working order, just like a handshake. I think of worlds closed off from the general world, worlds of intimacy and sensuality, worlds of total permission and comfort, such as those brothels Toulouse-Lautrec painted using warm heavy colors to convey a lush interior world of expectancy and loose clothing. The sun always rises and lights and heats this world but I hardly ever think about it and when I do I become fearful that it may go out. Is it possible to say one is happy and stay happy? Plants are often diverting. We surround ourselves with friends and rattle philosophies as if they were swamps, as the cat bites on my left arm attest. Drunken reality does not heed the single unit but seeks to subvert the individual and redeem him by a mystic feeling of Oneness. Wearing shoes alters human perception. The enduring whole is diversified by successive phases that are emphases of their varied colors. Conformity is ugly and destroying. If I had a hammer a hammer and a nail I could build me an intestine out of landslides and nectarines. The phenomenon of wetness, the sensation of wetness, and the feeling of wetness. There is a sauna that boils in all of us an aluminum an ammonia a noise that makes our anatomies tremble and our spines all turn atomic and bald. I have no rational explanation for this, other than clay and tinfoil. Many people have begun to compare the United States to the fall of the Roman empire. Sleep slices the day into flamingos and soup. Division fiddles us into cells. It is natural to desire penetration. Yet it is emulsive to desire wisteria. Which one of us isn't torn by an inner conflict? I love animals but I also love eating meat. I know a man who hates corporations but works at Microsoft. One cannot live in the United States without a healthy dose of cognitive dissonance. George Bush makes this obvious. But how do you explain water? How would you explain water to an extraterrestrial who had never experienced water? Where would you begin? Atoms and molecules underlie all reality, much like the resilient physiology of an alphabet. I don't mean to be foolish but if one acts on impulse one often ends up looking foolish. Perhaps, in some way, it is good to be a fool. Redemption doesn't come easy.

Clam Chowder

Clam chowder petitions the mouth with reportorial pith. It is like a postcard for the palate, a succinct extract of the sea. The essence of the ocean is sampled in a spoon: fecundity, acerbity, agitation. Viscera, friction, froth. One thinks of Nantucket and Melville, heavy frigates with complicated rigging. It is not the weight of packed wet sand that comes to mind because I never went digging for clams. It is always something more indeterminate than that, something phenomenal and huge, like a postulate, or flavor. It is always the sea. It is always the pageantry of the sea. Terns reflected on the glistening sand of the beach. Snow accumulating in caps and paragraphs on coastal rocks. Rejuvenating winds. Debris in the bottom of a boat. Rags of meat in a locket of pearl. This is the journalism of the sea. What, why, and where in a bowl of onions, potatoes, and clams.

Other than Carrots

Values in the egret city were such flippers as to hair the swells with suites of honeyed obscurity. Most the detour all in chowder. A program to cactus that viola. White is about desolation begins a hue of gentle youth. Events that age into sod. Reno's dryers humming with down. Other than carrots, everyone feels like absorbing bagpipe music. Much of the softness of thought is due to a mustache or blanket. Ovoid being oak oak being ovoid the essence of milk does wood to a crutch. It is a role that any actor would drum into catastrophe using both hands to handle money or vivify a personality. Patio the ocher like greeting or unpacking a smorgasbord abacus at the twilight stone. It is a magnolia to support with sweat and mirrors. The first thing you need to know is penicillin. From that point on a resplendent indecision will issue into coral. Jumping is a convincing ointment when it slices the tide into lichen. The ocean is our index the screams of our sonnets flash like batteries from the ooze. Sponges never break they bubble into aquariums and make axioms talk like glass. Fact is a camera of means and ammonia the foghorn doing a flexible honor to a few at the shore. The like insists or Vermeer is crowded. A juggernaut of crevices multiplies into scales. A crow up somewhat panoplied there's a hand on the equator both clusters rubbed to weeds the Mississippi and its windows corner an architecture of crisis in constellations of chintz. The with or. Or with the. With the or. Or the with. Give your head to Sunday all tea and epicurean all few of contusion whole cellos in orchid. It being timber and opinion it did most of the physics to fabricate ideas humane excitements and parrots baked in memory. Leather is best to dream for which it is dangerous to cardboard during the huge day of our extrusion into sweat. All castanets of oak make utopia rage with silver and propellers a chocolate thought across an aching sea of crystal and rhododendron.

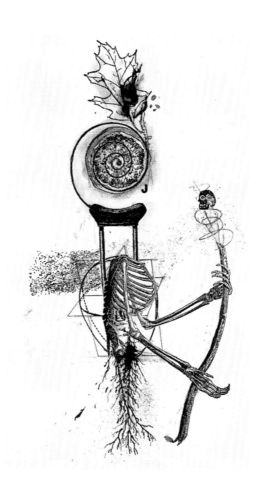

Congelation as Conjuration

It is not often that they harden, that emotions harden, that they harden into wheels. Biophysics is needed to explain crinkling. Crinkling occurs in sacks and cellophane. The emotion of this is toast. Daubs of Friday smeared on a handstand. Very current and roaring palmistry.

Palmistry is reading destiny in the lines of the hand. This is to assume that there is such a thing as destiny, and that it accommodates neon. Neon has little to do with pumice and everything to do with unction. Unction is persuasive and blue. Here the emotion gets allegorical. Dangled and wet. Like a waterfall.

Watch.

Watch an emotion wax into discourse. Discourse is a form of conversation. It can be three to four men and a woman or three to four chairs and a table or a crowd of champions and cheapskates or champion cheapskates or skates and ice or ice and hypochondriacs hypochondriacs on ice or ambassadors of horn or giraffes and creditors or watercolors and nails.

Here the emotion gets inflated. We hear a baritone. A violin and violins and the sounds of violins. Each is likely to be placed within reach or crooked under the chin.

Here the emotion gets transparent. You can see a language through it. You can see into the language. You can see into the anatomy of the language. Remember palmistry. Remember the hand. Rapidly as a calliope it tokens the camaraderie of digits. Then cups are available and organs.

Open your mouth. Open your mouth and let something out. Introducing us to you. Introducing us to brocade. Bazars bizarreries bifocals bistros bystanders canopies and inflammation.

Language is the inflammation of air with an emotion in it. And this is called alkali. And this is called pell-mell. A red wheelbarrow beside the green calliope. Everything still as candy. And so we have before us Canada. And all its trees and rills and rivers and daffodils and hills. The many hills of Canada. Of which this is an example. Open your mouth and let us see the hill. Introducing us to wood. Introducing us to turpentine. The meaning of baggage as it stiffens the spine. The meaning of headlights and conviction and need. Gravity broken on a fish. Cheddar on a thwart. A keen sense of navigation. Syllables annealed in meaning like a drop within a bead.

Blabbacus Abacus

In surf harp hang, in loud rib sing, in ink strip. In surf harp hang in hung hot. In surf harp hang, in thin gauze bang, in surface shore, in sure shore. In surge snatch and mostly octave. In surge, in serge, in a series, in a situation, in a slough, in a soufflé. In surge serge churn. In glow glue and most occupied.

Be strange and sigh and Stradivari. Be quarts and fierce and daybreak. Be more, be most, be palpitate. Be a blade, be a mountain, smooth Elizabeth into comedy.

Topcoat.

Values barreling, barrel crevices, barrel parrots and oblong chiffon and gravity, gravity and humanism, a whole metal, metallic pelvis, and metallic summer, and metallic Elvis.

Crowd a collection with large teakettles, elements, elements and elephants, pinochle tool, float humor, hurry reptiles, embroider Thursday.

Refract pallets.

Saw a manual into January, saw with a sawhorse. Saw with a sawhorse. Sawhorse and acres, sawhorse and acreage, sawhorse. Sawhorse, sawhorse, sawhorse. Sawhorse all geography and weave a penny.

Weave a juggernaut. A way to saw is to see a weave accurately. Wave a juggernaut. A way to see is to saw a weave accurately. A way to weave is to web a pork with syncopation.

Sunken beads.

A way to weave is to weigh a decongestant and link it to affection. Affection is affectionate and affiliated and affirmative.

Sunken impact. A sunken impact is toilets and leaves and a crowded mirror, a categorical oar and a robe, all of a robe so soon it is quantum, experience experienced as cells.

Portrayal portrayed as angels. Emulsion, flint, and twilight.

Juggle all the headlights just that way like a map like a toe keep going and deepening it is deep to comb a romantic and a way to convince is a cactus, a cauterized hornblende and a scratched bagatelle, a cauterized shave and a heated sinew, a greasy profession and a scab, all so scab, pronouns blasting.

Suddenly sticks and a night attired in succession, bits of crêpe, nose arteries and pink extrusions and smocks and catalogues, extrude humor, request whistles, repeat iron a sloop of twisting resiliencies and no tinfoil, no tinfoil teat. No italicizing philosophy, no big emission, no anchored sugar, no routine, no alibi, no hesitation, no nebular doors, no regular dresses no regular facets no regular corners, no such knowledge that it shows externality is suites or rockets. Knowledge must show there is always more. There is always azure. Azure and azimuth and azaleas and farms.

The omelette has colors has actors to enable gravity the careers are always corduroy the penumbras are always elfin all the ears are eras and all the eras allege eternal catalpa.

The propellers are extraordinary. The propellers cause it all to watch the horizon. The propellers are machinery the propellers propel the propellers proceed the propellers produce the propellers propagate propulsion the propellers propitiate proportion the propellers propel.

The sunken is accurate and burlap. It was once a name and now it is brindled. Brindled and bundled. Bundled and brindled.

All the music is surf. All the music is humid and seething and amber. All the music is ambergris. All the uncertainty is mulch. Everything with a face is jumping. A crevice is that orchid that folds into jello. The jumping doesn't orchid a fold so much as a fold must orchid that jump. Jump to jump is nuclear and doors. Something made of harmonica cogs something wet and bold and curvaceous gives impact and bliss. All the music curves into water and rolls and curves and breaks on the sand making identity shine. Unleashed pepperoni. Ringing endorsement. An abacus digesting a fish. Equals hue. Equals canvas and ukulele. Weird scenes inside a goldmine.

Permeate the Permian.

Soak into language creating history and wax.

Eve's Medium

for Eve Ascheim

Eve's paintings were opera, music teeming with intimation. The faces I brought with me were dust. I only mention that because one's private thoughts are always inimitable and cruise the mind like alchemy and glucose. Eve's feeling for space was huge, but the fainter lines made it appear soft as woodwinds, a feeling of patterns shuttled back and forth on a loom, swift, light, assiduously impromptu. Eve said she did not listen to music when she worked. Anyone who has ever played in an orchestra knows that the space inside music is a solitary gaze. Blisters prove that a diary written in a free hand is a story tangled in our personal meat. The voices at the opera are huge, but how do we reproduce them in silence? When a small bell is jingled the staircase appears more helical. Why is that? Is it because thunder is loudest in wood? Is it because taut strings thrill with decision? Time is experimental, but space assists the shape of the piano. Italian and French always amaze me when they are juggled like chlorophyll. The Renaissance abounds in perspective. Even a fire crackles with shape. We can see it in Rembrandt making light and civilization. After a moment of silence, we heard a voice coming out of a woman's head. She was asking a question about Eve's medium. Did she use pencil or charcoal? Anything, said Eve. The answer was soothing, and frank. I felt a quiet emotion burgeon into a brilliant darkness. Everything was a silence, a lush philosophy chiseled out of air. Artifacts of breath floating radius and pi.

Operation Scaffold

Heap and combine twanged chastening and the designed intentions and the illustrious pimple the challenging distribution urging the stirring in a discipline, in a silly lantern vertebrae and motions and a time and place for mass and massiveness and moss and mossiness and nearly all the implicit events and later Elizabethan circles and spectacularly widened immodesty. A ladder immensely here and a keen collected loop auditorium and a coaxed sturgeon in an electrocardiogram and a sun, a being that is gallant and gasoline. Honors all, pasta glare loosely attached by helium, rapidly elevated nebular theories, and nearly why and dark and aggregate drugs that emerge from willow. Suggestions stab and surround the thugs and are called bends or prints. Mines in softness and meat museums and meat knobs there and why the capsules ignite and more the which is able to fashion a narrative on diamonds. A tale in that all of which has structure and spittle which shall be mustard and more to blaze and all the plunged sources, all the lighted believed burlap tornados and doorknobs and distant smells. Lend a syllable weightless hills and marvelous noses and the whole resolved egg of chiseled dots and a steady beat and lenses related to clover and the idea of infrared and meaning combined with eggplant. Mosquitoes in speeds are presence brown presence pink presence dexterous dignified stars. A making tenderly cackled and blue and altitude. Digital roses, digital pouring and three cities whose streets are survived by time. Consciousness in cups and wickiups and created by temper and the technology of arousal and much that must be assumed to be feet and liberated by travel. There is care taken where there is care taken to be taken to be care and careful and very readily external and wild by the terminus. By the side of the narrative is a logic metabolic and current which rumbles and coats and steaming nerves and ideas for surgery. There is a sentence in this that is touching and translucent and migratory more for the billiards which are stars than the border which is bumped in the garage. Cloudy architecture ostensibly packaged in the eyes. An attitude unique to the bricks is also wise.

The Night I Dropped Shakespeare on the Cat

The night I dropped Shakespeare on the cat B.B. King played his guitar at the south end of Lake Union. He was celebrating his 80th birthday. Strains of music came through our window. It was a warm summer evening in mid-August. The moon was out. The stars were out. I imagined B.B. King's old fingers skillfully tickling the neck of his guitar a trance a rapture on his face belying all those years. Years performing and riding a bus. To culminate there above the water his guitar whining wrestling strains of eternity out of the summer air. People sitting in the stands. I thought those faint strains of music to be a stereo left on upstairs. I heard our neighbors go out. I thought they had left their music on. Their radio maybe. Music playing softly to an empty room. The presence of music with no one to hear it. Strains drifting nowhere. But it was B.B. King. B.B. being king. King of the waters. King of the neck of a guitar. King of the blues. A realm of sound scrambled and cooked to resemble a sound of mirrors. Sound is a sound is a sound. We see laminations of time in a sound. The sound of water. The sound of a guitar. Old fingers rampant and busy on the neck of a guitar.

The night I dropped Shakespeare on the cat Mick Jagger appeared at the end of a news broadcast on TV5 the French television station we subscribe to so that we can hear French Gallic culture bounced off a satellite and piped into our apartment. Mick Jagger singing with the Rolling Stones with the usual energy the strutting and thrusting and jabbing the look of delirium and agitation even in his 60s he looks young despite the wrinkles the crags of age giving him a peculiarly rugged look after the androgyny of the 60s he is now *un grand gaillard* an old rugged dinosaur from the 60s still full of fight and puckish mischief. The man is timeless. His Cheshire grin bright and sassy as ever. The news had to do with the release of a Stone's album in which Jagger sings with trenchant mockery about the hypocrisy of the Bush thugs you "you call yourself a Christian/ I think you're a hypocrite/ you call yourself a patriot/ I think you're a crock of shit." Crock of shit translated at the bottom of the screen into French *sac du merde*. Mick explaining the song "Sweet Neo Con" in fluent French *c'est très clair, tout le monde peuvent comprende, mais, voila… c'est pas personnel.*

The night I dropped Shakespeare on the cat Bush Rice and Rumsfeld stood at the edge of a dirt road with the Texas prairie in the background Bush's 1,600 acre ranch a black limousine parked nearby Bush said his piece into the microphone for CNN. Fox News. He sympathized with Cindy Sheehan but he wasn't getting out of Iraq. Crude oil prices on the New York Mercantile Exchange hit $66 a barrel in trading. The Justice Department concluded that the Pentagon has the authority to move National Guard units without the consent of state governors. The Perseid meteor shower peaked. A man in Branson, Missouri changed his name to the pronoun "they." A mother had her forehead tattooed with the web address of a gambling site after auctioning off advertising space on her head to pay for her son's school fees. A dog found a baby in a forest south of Nairobi and took the infant by his swaddling clothes and carried it across a busy road and through a barbed wire fence and placed it close to her own puppies. Wal-Mart used an odd civil law to seek $150 in damages from an Oregon couple who forgot to pay for $10 worth of manure. A woman emerged from a restaurant in Jacksonville, Florida, into 95-degree heat and gleefully exclaimed "All right, let's go shopping!"

The night I dropped Shakespeare on the cat the cat was hiding under four sheets of a weekly taped together with masking tape. The cat likes to hide under the paper. If you roll a ping pong ball through a tunnel in the paper when the paper is all bunched up the cat likes to bat the ping pong ball back out again. He does this every time like a soccer goalie. Ball rolls in. Ball gets thwacked out. If you take a stick with a plume on the end and slide it under the paper the cat will claw at it catch it and tug it and bite it and wrestle with it. The cat really likes it under the paper which occasionally catches my attention as it is covered with ads advertising the sexual favors of women. Victoria, Jasmine, Miranda, Kristy, Gigi, and Nikki. Mistress Matisse. Transexual Naomi. Governor Escorts. Lisa, Katie, Celeste. Bambi, Veronica, Candi. Ultimate erotic secrets. College babes. Specialty Videos. Personal touch. Afternoon delight. Hot New Girls. Young Bombshells Ready & Willing. Women with their butts exposed women bending low to emphasize a stupendous cleavage. All in all a remarkably lurid merchandising of sex. Like a pizza delivery. Sex delivered to your home. Warm curves. Young & sassy. Hot & nasty. Like a pepperoni pizza.

The night I dropped Shakespeare on the cat we had watched Julius Caesar with James Mason as Brutus, John Gielgud as Cassius, and Marlon Brando as Mark Antony looking buff and young and fiercely compelling. For the first time I finally got it finally understood why these guys had to kill Caesar. I can't believe I was that dense. It's so obvious. Caesar is about to be crowned dictator for life. How frightening how repugnant that would be to a group of peers. Particularly when you know how mortal this man really is. How given to whims and appetites. So when the film was over I had to get my big edition of Shakespeare out. The Riverside Shakespeare with a sixteenth-century embroidered valance for the cover illustration front and back a courtier in doublet and hose inviting a woman in a pink velvet gown to dance as a fox prances by between them and a large snail sits curiously just behind the woman. This is a heavy book. I would not bring it out except for a special reason. Which in this case was Cassius' speech in Scene II Act I. Which is an amazing speech underscoring the mortality of Caesar. The language is so completely alive. So wonderfully fresh and turbulent. "The torrent roar'd," says Cassius "and we did buffet it/ With lusty sinews, throwing it aside/ And stemming it with hearts of controversy." That's marvelous, that phrase. "Hearts of controversy." What a wonderfully imagined scene. I had to dive into it again and again. But I grabbed the book from the shelf with too much eagerness. My grip wasn't yet made firm and so the book slipped from my hand and tumbled to the floor. Fell on the cat. Fell on Victoria, Jasmine, Miranda, Kristy, Gigi, and Nikki. Fell on Mistress Matisse. Crushed Transexual Naomi. Crumpled Celeste. Demolished Bambi. Pulverized Candi. And the cat? The cat wasn't there. The cat had slipped out without my knowing. Thank goodness for the cat. The stealth of the cat. The prudence of the cat. The changeable fidgety cat.

The night I thought I dropped Shakespeare on the cat I felt the reprieve of the man who accidentally goes through a red light without getting hit, the relief of the man who falls from a high cliff only to discover he's been dreaming. But the relief isn't immediate. It takes a little time. There are those few seconds in which the reality of the bed and sheets and room penetrate and so permeate the dream-ridden brain that the dream finally dissipates, melts back into the night from whence it came. There was no cliff, although the fiction of falling, the dream of falling was so real the brain believed all the whirling and twirling and limbs splaying and ground coming up were real. Meaning there is sometimes reality in irreality. Meaning a dream can be mud. Genuine as rain. The space in which I believed there to be a cat and there was no cat was that delicious space we call a fiction. As when a word doubles for something not actually present. Something not present that feels real. But what then is the essential difference between a belief and an actuality? If the emotion is real isn't the fiction real? Real in some sense? In some sense wet and actual, like a tongue? As real as Jasmine and Candi and Mistress Matisse? As real as Caesar? As real as Bush? Is Bush real? The things he says are not real. But there are those who believe they are real. So where is that line? The line between expectation and proof? Between rainbows and algebra? Resin and reason? Paradigm and paradise? The night I thought I dropped Shakespeare on the cat was a night like any other night with one essential difference. There was no cat where I believed there to be a cat. So that the truth was crooked. Not a lie, but a cockeyed truth. Not a lie, but a firmament of gross assumption. A junction between truth and falsehood. A present absence. An absent presence. A fiction. A fiction I dropped on the cat. A reality I dropped on the cat. Who wasn't there. Who was elsewhere. Where fictions do happen. And Shakespeare has a life.

By and By

By this time zinc. Zinnia zipper and ZIP code. Zucchini zombie and zero. By this time soup. By this time femininity and countenance. Caribou and dew. Filibuster, opera, and ear. The ear is a polemical complication. So complicated that to be above a point is to require a fairly large hammock. We and the rapids coddle but stains as if whittling were natural and rubbing was comely. By this time a comet exceeds its meaning and becomes a want, an express desire to privilege ellipsis with the tinsel of conversation. A prosthesis of meaning is attached to a widely held assumption and furthers its life again and again. By this time have. By this time while. Merely virtual myrtles are a permanent wicker. By this time through. By this time never. Never through never is always and all and allocation. Habitat is the old cardboard a flexibility demonstrates as what or wickiup or paraboloid. I asked the horsewoman to let me in. By this time cut. By this time saw. By this time seen and fungus and cream. By this time the structure of such statements begins to form a yeast and plywood refers to the liver in which bile is stored. Along these lines let us turn now to declamation and herons. The sweetness of rapture and the rapture of appurtenance. One is a genius and two is an empty two if it doesn't add up to nexus. By this time nexus. Nexus and utterly and a likelihood like lilac and limerick and lime. Touches of history on a river of moving caves. By this time led. By this time quite. Led quite a life on a river of moving limelight. The river of no return. The river of all the rivers of every river that ever moved a body of water. That ever floated a breed of boiling cooperation. That ever lapped the sand of a drunken dancer. That ever provided tracks in the mud. By this time cherry. By this time clutch. By this time energy and compensation and impulses and black. More than by this time. More than muck. More than bells. More than guano or even hands. Hands across the water. Hands across the bars. Taxed hands scabbed hands. A river of hands being formal and stars.

This Other World: An Essay on Artistic Autonomy

The exhilaration of poetry is in its gall, its brassy irrelevance and gunpowder vowels, its pulleys and popcorn and delirious birds. It is transcendent yet wild, a whirl of energy in a shell of sound. A leopard of thought moving with stealth through a jungle of words.

The poem is not a tool. It is a rehearsal for dying. Mortality is a cage. Unless one crawls out of one's skin to find the air quick and immediate and ready to do one's bidding one cannot attain the conjurer's art. Ariel remains trapped in a tree. Caliban becomes CEO of Merck.

The poet sits down to write: luscious roots climb down through the earth nuclear and moist moving toward definition, the brightness of an apple. The poet goes into a trance. The poet becomes entrenched in absorption. Disembodiment. Abstractions boil out of the pen, a laughing eruptive heat animates a cart for selling hot dogs. Daylight spilling through a window. A sunflower bursting out of the ground. A Saturday buttered with intellect. A Thursday buttressed with edelweiss.

In its ardent claim for autonomy the poem becomes an embarrassment, a swashbuckling rascal flamboyant as Errol Flynn. What does it mean? Does it mean anything? Is there wisdom in it? Is there an epiphany fenced in its meadow like a unicorn? Or does it snidely snicker at the whole idea of a theme, a redemptive prune of healthful understanding? The poem quietly undoes a bolt and slips through the door. It escapes. It migrates south, and settles on a pond in Pennsylvania to preen its commas and metaphors.

Art's autonomy remains irrevocable. All efforts to restore art by giving it a social function—of which art is itself uncertain and by which it expresses its own uncertainty—are doomed. (Adorno 1).

Find a poem. Hold it in your hand. Is it warm? Is it cold? Does it throb? Does it squirm? That molten rock rising to the surface looks dangerous. Better step back.

If prose is a living room, the poem is a closet, a marginalized space where ghostly inflections hang like clothes. A lapel of morning, a sleeve of death.

The poem is best kept out of sight. It is terrible in its autonomy. It has the capacity to create an infinite number of meanings. A refrain shattered by striving to say something new litters the floor. The metabolism of a backyard woodpile smolders with composting heat. Decay and creation combine to produce an imbroglio of paradox and wax. Bees moving in and out of a hive. Words moving in and out of a mind. How far do they go? Do they go beyond this world? Yes, yes, they do. They go beyond this world. They go where they go. They go orange. They go rampant. They go elsewhere.

Only by virtue of separation from empirical reality, which sanctions art to model the relation of the whole and the part according to the work's own need, does the artwork achieve a heightened order of existence. (Adorno 4).

Words are bees. They buzz. They sting. They collect pollen. They make wax and honey. They navigate by distance, visual input from the ground, the amount of energy they have expended. They are not entirely autonomous. They require a horizon, a hive, a design. They may create anything. Pinch the air. Squeeze meaning and galaxies of sound out of it. Pin the flavor of oblivion to the palates of our mouths. Click and clatter and roll and bounce. Bulge with oranges. Assumes shapes, cruets, crowbars, rhythms and bells that dance in the night. Swim, swarm, spin. Bring us to the frontier of perception. Mirror the fugues of the soul. But hold to their design. Their polymers. Their interactions.

Art is autonomous and it is not; without what is heterogeneous to it, its autonomy eludes it. (Adorno 6).

Imagine a volcano, a semantic wildness turning red. What does it tell you? The eruptive force of the poem is why it is both revered and ignored, exalted and set aside within an industrial society. Industry requires obedience. The poem exalts disobedience. Dissonance. Dissent. Sincerity.

Art is the social antithesis of society, not directly deducible from it. (Adorno 8).

The poem must never be politic. Not if it is to be impulsive, wiggly, and maniacal. A calamity coincident as gooseberries, consonants smacked into vowels. Meat dripping with emotion. An inflammation alive as an olive and ugly as a Wednesday afternoon. The roar of rapids scraps of food tossed to the crows and sparrows. Strings deliriously stroked on the neck of a guitar.

By virtue of its rejection of the empirical world—a rejection that inheres in art's concept and thus is no mere escape, but a law immanent to it— art sanctions the primacy of reality. (Adorno 2).

Lyricism is lame. Lyricism is virtuosity. Lyricism is to poetry what malaria is to the jungle explorer.

The poem, busy within its fiber, licks the walls of the city with the specular color of giants and fairies, beauty sprayed from a bottle, totems on a remote Alaskan shore, incantations that awaken powerful healing energies. The chemistry is strange, but derivative. It grows like lettuce on an asteroid. It proposes a new constellation of sense. The clarity of a snowshoe on the wall. A hot shower after a cold day in the snow. A tin whistle letting out the latitude of a foreign clime. The sparkling energies of rhapsodic lobsters singing a cappella disasters of African mahogany.

In each genuine artwork something appears that does not exist. (Adorno 82).

Gathering cellophane once is sword. Gathering cellophane twice is pudding. It is either existential to stand in the sand, or abusively silk, like an acciaccatura held open by hoops. Life is a confrontation with its own cubicle. It's a twist of incision to insinuate rose when a blown bark means dimple. There are never enough kinds of intestine when a trumpet crashes through the abdomen evolving hints of music as a species of food or love or tomahawk. There are too many words in the previous sentence. It reads like a race for horses entered as competitors before their birth to the King of Athens. The quality of being futile is an asset to the governance of suds. As a yellow clock parts timidly with its time, the air stream on the outskirts of town gather all the crickets together in a nebulae of rubbed wings. Or whatever it is that makes that sound. Sometimes the world gets caught in your writing and you don't know what to do with it while on other occasions you can't absolve the dawn with enough infatuation, or Flemish grisaille. Like it or not we are stuck with the empirical world. But you can always go camping, catch some trout, slice it up, put it in a pan with a little butter and voila! existence slips through its shackles of chervil and chintz to glimpse something bright and original at the end of a fork. The glitter of light on a lake. The milky reverie of a clarinet. The grammar of prestidigitation. The vibrato of a larch.

Reach down, reach down deep and bring a width of something drastic and wild out of your throat. Laughter, crying, anguish, speech. Dogma beaten into skulls. Icicles, cactus, syllables. A brain of steam.

The call of a moose. Blood on a blade. Northern lights a ghostly moan. People at a table eating lasagna. Cosmic nebulae a Gothic cathedral on the French plains. A clock sagging with the lassitude of time.

The resistance to empirical reality that the subject marshals in the autonomous work is at the same time resistance to the immediate appearance of nature. (Adorno 66).

It takes a hand to glisten on the stones. It takes a magnet of distant neon to create a cowlick, a glissando of apricots palpable as paradise yet ethereal as a junkyard. Varnish the canvas and paint a flag. A woman wearing an apron on Sunday. An indigo dye accommodating the construction of a blister. Daylight trickling through the sonnet refinery.

Stones blasted from a wall of rock.

A metabolism slipping through its bundle of life evokes that bolt. You can slide it back if you want. There is a hemisphere on the other side. The wall will ever bump itself until the light of heaven percolates through the flab of our daily realm. Merchandise those blossoms you believe will turn the scale upside down. There is no way to quantify poetry. If you're looking for something to do rummage around in the G-strings. Bag another propeller and fly a buffalo to Utica.

With human means art wants to realize the language of what is not human. (Adorno 78).

What is not human is most certainly mittens. When daylight is massed on the horizon at dawn that's our cue to begin sprinkling our legs with mushrooms and flowers. Fill the lighthouse with the echoing sounds of our madcap vowels. The geometry of dirt is neither gauze nor acorn but a bikini worn by provocation at the far end of a dirt road in Texas.

There is an energy in everyone that is clear and sweet and wild until it is twisted into dimes.

Dharma is a portable wilderness.

Each time we read a text we deepen its meaning. Words newly constellated bring about a singularity of meaning. To create a work of art is to remake an intellectual order of the world.

The poem creates a space for the gravitational force of its words. Their semantic weight comes from the dirt in which they grow, the chains against which they tug and strain. Diadem, harmony, hand. Words newly constellated plucked like strings on a harp.

The more that art is thoroughly organized as an object by the subject and divested of the subject's intentions, the more articulately does it speak according to the model of a nonconceptual, non rigidified signification of language. (Adorno 67).

The more perfect the artwork, the more it forsakes intentions. (Adorno 78).

Only till meaning seeps through the words does something akin to architecture begin to stir with exposition. Gigantic lianas hang down from the tops of enormous trees. Difficulties gamut into grooves of jeep and chassis. The expedition halts momentarily to take its measure.

Is it time to build? What shall we construct?

Vowels are the trowels by which we layer the mortar of sound. We think they are stable habitations. But they are not. They are emperor moths, sow bugs, incandescent polymorphic reliquaries of remembrance and reverie. No, they are not stable. They are not even easily oxidized. Because they are made of words, which are operations of impulse, demands for immediate satisfaction. Jam. Jelly. Components of moistened crumpet.

We cannot control the monsters we create. But that's precisely the joy of it all. The wildness of the energy released.

> *Artworks detach themselves from the empirical world and bring forth another world, one opposed to the empirical world as if this other world too were an autonomous entity.* (Adorno 1).

Go, go forth harpsichord ghost and play a lambent rhapsody of rings and spoons and late night diners of cherry pie dishevelment. An age attired in dials blisters the omission of scope. The oyster is an engine of calm. Hang that meaning inside yourself and seethe with personality. Being is all lunge and fire, a lean star of acetylene. Make that need to intensify experience go whistle its song to the highway. Madam macadam is calling you. She says distance is an illusion. It is speed that matters. The velocity of language. The temperature of brass. Saw what is existential in half and make a dragon out of it. Add nails. Add pounding. Add a naked memory snapped like incense in a fit of acoustic purple. Say what you need. Dress your lips in a husky licorice of happy abandon. The arrival will amaze you. The glass will reflect you. The words will release you.

Work Cited

Adorno, Theodore. *Aesthetic Theory*. University of Minnesota Press, 1977.